At Sea *with* God

A Spiritual Guidebook to the Heart and Soul

Take a lively and enjoyable spiritual journey with Margaret Silf, one of the most accessible and inviting Christian spiritual writers today. Let this experienced guide help you navigate your way through difficult times, steer your boat through rocky waters, and chart a course through deeper intimacy with God. You'll enjoy the trip almost as much as the joyful destination.

James Martin, S.J.
Author of *My Life with the Saints*

Leave it to Margaret Silf to come up with a lovely metaphor for the spiritual journey, a trip to sea! With her usual insight and attention to the concrete details of life she leads readers on the wonderful journey that God creates us for. Readers of Silf's earlier works will not be disappointed.

William A. Barry, S.J.
Author of *Paying Attention to God*

Keep your spiritual bearings anywhere with this brilliantly insightful and practical guidebook! With tenderness and challenge, Margaret Silf helps the spiritual navigator chart a steady course on life's unpredictable seas. Through compelling stories and her own dynamic life experience, she teaches us to trust ourselves, to explore untried sources of strength, to rely on those who love us, and to always lean into God.

Rev. Holly Whitcomb
Author of *Seven Spiritual Gifts of Waiting*

With the freshness of expression and depth of personal experience that made *Inner Compass* such a remarkable book, Margaret Silf now unpacks the metaphor of being at sea with God and uses it to help us reflect on the spiritual journey. You don't have to have ever been in a boat to appreciate her insights. It is a book for all who seek to know what it is to be held by God as they pass through the waters of life.

Dr. David G. Benner, PhD, CPsych
Distinguished Professor of Psychology and Spirituality,
Psychological Studies Institute, Atlanta
Author of *The Gift of Being Yourself,*
Desiring God's Will, and *Surrender to Love*

At Sea *with* God

A Spiritual Guidebook to the Heart and Soul

Margaret Silf

SORIN BOOKS   Notre Dame, Indiana

First published in 2003 by
Darton, Longman and Todd Ltd
1 Spencer Court
140-142 Wandsworth High Street
London SW18 4JJ

www.sorinbooks.com

ISBN-10 1-933495-11-1 ISBN-13 978-1-933495-11-8

Cover and text design by David Scholtes.

Printed and bound in the United States of America.

Library of Congress Cataloging-in-Publication Data
Silf, Margaret.
At sea with God : a spiritual guidebook to the heart and soul / Margaret Silf.
    p. cm.
Includes bibliographical references.
ISBN-13: 978-1-933495-11-8
ISBN-10: 1-933495-11-1
1. Spiritual retreats--Christianity. 2. Spiritual life--Christianity. I. Title.
BV5068.R4S56 2008
269'.6--dc22

                                        2007048765

Contents

Angel nor saint have I seen,

but I have heard the roar of the western sea

and the isle of my heart is in the midst of it.

—St. Columba

Introduction

"At sea!" What, I wonder, do these words suggest to you? In these islands we are surrounded by it. We may hate it, or love it. When I let the words "at sea" float through my mind and memory and imagination, all kinds of reactions arise. I remember times of my life when I have felt completely "at sea" amid unpredictable, or even hostile, circumstances, without a clue as to what to do or how to respond. The words can evoke fear in me, in the light of such memories, but also gratitude that, after all, I didn't drown. Then again, there are images of awesome beauty—times when the waters were calmer, and seemed to invite me to unfurl my sails confidently and let the great expanse of life draw me beyond all my known horizons. I feel awe, and a profound sense of wonder that the "seas" can be so vast, yet so supportive of the tiny boat I call my life. This evokes a different kind of gratitude—a feeling of joyous amazement that I am a part of it all, however minuscule.

The sea is a source of terror and glory: the coastal waters that lap around our familiar islands; the ocean waters that beckon us beyond ourselves; the provider of food and the dwelling place of monsters. It has the potential to engulf us, and the power to carry us, rejoicing, to regions beyond our wildest dreams.

And what about those other two little words, "with God"? What might "God" mean for us? Or as Jesus might have put it, "Who is God for you?"

If I were to try to answer such a question (and any answer would have to remain forever highly provisional, since "God" is always going to be mystery, beyond name or face, image or definition) then some of the reactions that might come to mind would also be about "glory" and "terror," about being held by someone I can't see or understand, about sailing over waters that give me what I need to stay alive but also make me face my personal depths, where both my demons and my angels live. But I think the sense of awe, and the desire to sail beyond what we can see and understand, can prevail over our

1

fears. If it were not so, I wouldn't be engaged on what we often call "a spiritual journey," and neither would you.

So this book is an invitation to make a voyage of the heart and soul and see what's there to discover. It has nothing to do with creed or doctrine, but everything to do with the lived experience of being "at sea" in the events and relationships of life, and the intuition that we don't make such a voyage alone. It is a voyage that involves all creation, and an adventure that can lead us closer to the core of our being and to the core of all being.

For me, perhaps, to be alive is to be "at sea" (in all its shifting moods and movements), and to be, at all, is to be held in being by a wholeness and fullness of Life and Love that I can only call God.

Before we set sail I'd like to express my love and gratitude to all those who have sailed with me through the years—especially to my parents, the late Irene and Bernard Ashton, to my husband Klaus and daughter Kirstin, who have shared the best and the worst of the weather and not given up on me, to Brian McClorry, S.J., and Gerry Hughes, S.J., who have guided my course through violent storms and over endless horizons of discovery, and to those "soul friends" who are always willing to share the wonder of the distant vision, help bale out the bilge water, and keep me hanging on in there when the weather turns foul.

I am particularly indebted to two friends, Ann Beazer and Chris Lane, who have helped to "ground" my metaphorical journey in the reality of the Solent waters on board their boat *Otter II*, and have most kindly sifted through the draft of this book to remove the worst errors of nautical fact from its pages. Whatever howlers remain are down to me and my deplorable lack of hands-on experience when it comes to manning real boats in real seas. It takes a special kind of sailor to convince you that seasickness is a "good bonding experience," and to bear with your incompetence in getting into a life jacket. Thank you, Ann and Chris, for your patience, enthusiasm, and sea-wisdom, and for the sheer fun of our days at sea with you and Jenny.

And thank you, too, to those who took part in three early "At Sea with God" retreats, at St. Antony's Priory, Durham (March 2001), Highmoor Hall, Oxfordshire (February 2002), and Loyola Hall on Merseyside (April 2002), and who have enriched the journey so much by sharing their own discoveries and insights. My special thanks are due to those who kindly gave permission for something of their experience to be included in these pages. I am also greatly indebted to Marion Jepson, who has been a dear friend and companion, first to my parents and now to me, and who has encouraged me so much with her wisdom and her comments on the manuscript of this book.

Finally, this is a moment to say "Farewell" to our beloved ship's cat, Mustafa, who has, sadly, sailed beyond the horizon. Whoever God is, God is certainly big enough to embrace a little creature who generated so much love in his twelve years on Earth.

Boats get launched after the boatyard has finished building them. Books do things the other way round. They get built after the author has done her bit, and I would like to thank the "builders" of this book: my colleagues at Darton, Longman and Todd in London, especially Kathy Dyke and Helen Porter, for all their work in bringing the book to the shelves; and Brendan Walsh, for his unflagging encouragement and sensitive and challenging editing.

I was once reminded that the Ark was built by an amateur, but the *Titanic* was built by professionals. This is a book written by an amateur, for amateurs, in the art of sailing life's waters by a Christian compass. We are all in the same boat. We are all "at sea." But my experience, and yours, might give us reason to believe that we are not at sea alone. We are at sea with each other and with God. Journey well!

CHAPTER

1

The Boat

Incredible journeys in little boats! They weave through human history like living strands that won't lie down and be forgotten. They fire our imagination and stir up our spirit of adventure. We catch ourselves reaching for the oars, testing the wind, sniffing the salt air, and wondering, deeply, about the voyage of our own little life.

Legend has it that a Celtic saint called Brendan made an epic voyage from the west coast of Ireland, reaching America a thousand years before Christopher Columbus. Did he really do it? And if so, in what kind of a boat? The seafaring craft of the time would have been of primitive design, constructed from skins stretched over a wooden frame. Could he have crossed the Atlantic in such a fragile little currach, or coracle? There was only one way to find out. After all the researching and debating, all the calculations and conjectures, the only way to be sure was to try to do the same thing. A boat was carefully constructed, using only the techniques and materials known to have been available at the time, and a second crossing was attempted. Those who believed Brendan really did it had to put their feet where their mouths were, get into their boat, and set sail. They embarked upon what became known as the Brendan Voyage.

South Sea folk memory also holds fast to the story that the Polynesian Islands were first visited by adventurers who crossed the Pacific Ocean from the land where the sun rises (South America) more than 1,500 years ago, and carried their civilization to the Pitcairns, Easter Island, Tahiti, and Samoa. But how? They had no boats! Or so it was thought. Thor Heyerdahl couldn't take no for an answer. They may not have had boats, but they had coastal fishing rafts made from balsa wood logs. Could such makeshift rafts have crossed the 4,000 miles or so that separated South America from the Polynesian Islands? For Heyerdahl, the question wouldn't lie down. And so began the *Kon-Tiki* expedition, in which, with five companions and a parrot, he crossed the Pacific on a replica raft of balsa wood logs lashed together with ropes, trusting in a flimsy sail and the trade winds to carry them to their destination. Their journey has become a legend. Like the Brendan Voyagers, Heyerdahl knew that the only way to find out whether the incredible journeys of the distant past could really have happened was actually to get in the boat and sail.

There is something in this willingness to put to sea and discover for ourselves whether the old stories can possibly be true that resonates with our Christian journeying. Millions of people believe that a special person, with divine power and huge charisma, lived and died two thousand years ago, and in some mysterious way still lives on in those who believe in him. The evidence is persuasive. But do we trust it enough to get in the boat and put to sea?

When I think of Brendan's little boat, I can't help noticing its similarity to the vessel I call my life. I too, like you, consist mainly of a skin stretched over a rather flimsy framework—not of wood but of bone, muscle, and tendon. My "boat" may be slightly better padded than Brendan's, but the design is otherwise much the same. My boat, too, is designed for an adventure—a voyage of discovery. It isn't intended to sit in the boatyard all my days, or to bask in safe moorings.

Or, like Heyerdahl's raft, my life is a bit like those nine balsa wood logs, roped together, floating along, often in uncomfortable intimacy with the "sea" of my life's circumstances. He describes the sensation of sailing this raft as being "like lying on the back of a large breathing animal," yet the raft rides the waves with unexpected flexibility and resilience.

There is a secret energy in me, too, as in Brendan and in Heyerdahl and his companions, that yearns to be under sail and away beyond the horizon. I am not just a cog in the world's wheel. I am a living cell in the thrilling dynamism of the evolution of life itself, both physical and spiritual. My own boat's journey will—if I let it—open up some new part of the cosmic vision that only my personal voyage can reveal. It will, in some mysterious way, take me back to the source of my being, and take me forward to who I am truly meant to be. Yet I am one of a fleet of millions upon millions of human lives—those who have already sailed beyond the horizon, those who are struggling and rejoicing even now on the high seas of life, and those whose vessels are not yet built, yet wait in tomorrow's secret places for their own tide to carry them into life. And each and every one of us has a voyage to make, a vision to discover, a new fragment of an old dream to give to creation.

So, do we believe it? Do we believe we are more than a cupful of carbon and a few liters of water? Will we put our feet where our mouths are, and sail the boat, trusting that such a frail little vessel will actually make the distance?

This book is an invitation to just such an adventure.

The shape of your boat

What kind of boat might represent this life we are living? We have established that its basic construction is skin stretched over a framework of bone and muscle, and brought to life by an invisible energy that begins at conception and keeps us going until we draw our final breath. But no two human boats are alike. We are all a fusion of body, mind, and soul. We are all created from the matter of the universe and enlivened by what we might truthfully call divine energy. But built upon these basic properties, each of us is a unique vessel, sailing our own course and called to become uniquely who we are.

Our life is like a voyage of discovery. Every moment is an opportunity to discover something of the mystery of God and God's desire for our personal living and growing. Every day is a chance to discover new ways of cooperating with the coming of God's Kingdom on our planet Earth. The circumstances of our own lives are the vessel, and the only vessel, in which we can make this voyage of discovery. What is our personal boat like? What kind of vessel might it be?

Reflect

You might like to begin this voyage by pondering the shape and function of the particular boat that is you. If you can imagine your life, and all you are, as a boat, what kind of boat would it be?

Is it, for example, a passenger liner, a cargo boat, a tug, or a fishing boat?

Or perhaps a lifeboat, an explorer ship, a galleon, or a submarine?

Or maybe a rowing boat, a sailing dinghy, a racing yacht, or a coracle?

Maybe it's even a canal barge, a man-of-war, an ice-breaker, or an ark.

Is it sailing the high seas, or paddling up inland waterways, or dabbling around on the pond in the park? All these places are equally good and proper places to be, depending on what type of boat you are and where your voyage has so far taken you.

Is it struggling, or cruising along nicely? Or, more likely, an unpredictable mixture of the two?

Are you alone in it, or one of a crew? Are you mainly a solitary soul who prefers to paddle your own canoe? Or are you a gregarious individual, tending to view your life and your circumstances more in the nature of a team effort alongside those around you? Just notice. Don't make any judgments.

Simply enjoy a few minutes of fantasy, while you meet up, in your imagination, with your boat. This is going to be your partner in the adventure of life. How do you feel about it? And, of course, the kind of boat you are may well change over the course of your life, or you may feel that the kind of boat you are varies in the different roles and relationships of your life.

Whatever boat comes to mind may be suggesting something very specific and personal about the particular ways in which God is inviting you to make your life's journey—ways that are just right for your personality and within your own circumstances.

The boatyard

Boats don't just happen. They are made, and the making is a skilled and creative task. Your life, likewise, didn't just happen, whatever the particular circumstances of your birth may have been. Long generations—indeed billions of millennia—of evolution and growth have gone into the making of you, just as long generations of boatbuilding skills have gone into the creation of every new vessel.

The boatyard can mean many things. Certainly it is about your personal gene pool. The pattern of your becoming was being shaped long before any of your known ancestors walked the earth, or before human beings walked the earth at all. You have certain characteristics that are programmed into your physical and mental being. You might like to reflect on what good gifts you feel you have inherited genetically from your forbearers. And notice, without any judgment, any less desirable characteristics that have come along with the package.

But the boatyard has to do with more than your physical makeup. It has to do with everything that has contributed to making you who you are—your parents and family, your own story, the whole human story, and the story of the universe itself.

When you reflect on those who are related to you, who have preceded you on this journey of exploration we call life, you may see other kinds of boats. For example, I feel (at this point in my journey at least) that my boat is an explorer boat. But when I look back a few generations, I can see other vessels in the family fleet. There are several lifeboats in my boatyard, who have relished the risk of being alive and defending the lives of others. And there are a couple of tankers, whose main role in life has been to supply the needs of others, sometimes at the expense of their own needs. There is at least one trading ship, plying the oceans of the world and probing the boundaries of new lands. And, yes, there are a couple of gunboats! How does this help me to become familiar with my own boat? Well, some of these other vessels from my history will have left their traces on how my own boat came to be how it is. It can be fascinating to do a spot of detective work (without becoming obsessive about it) on these traces of "otherness."

Of course, the boatyard isn't manned solely by our forebearers, or those who share our family tree. What about the people who have influenced your life significantly? Whether they are still alive, or long dead, remember who they were, and notice what gifting—what special flavor—they have added to the mix of possibilities from which you are emerging. One of my dearest friends is probably a submarine. He goes deep and you never quite know where he is going to turn up. Another is a self-confessed coracle, who teaches me a great deal about the spirit of pilgrimage. And I was deeply touched by a lady who once shared with me her feelings of being a tugboat. She was just about to retire from a life of working as a midwife, and she was longing to continue to be the kind of person who gently accompanies and guides others through the straits of transition and assists their rites of passage.

Another thing that the boatyard speaks to me about is tradition. Tradition is what has taught us how to become the boat we are, and has inspired us with the desire to sail the oceans of life. As we move into a closer focus on our spiritual journeying, many of us will find that an important aspect of the boatyard is the spiritual tradition that has formed and nurtured us. This book is written from roots deep within the Christian tradition, though I hope that it will also speak to spiritual pilgrims from other faiths or from none. For Christians, it is the Christian tradition that has told us the Christ-story, and given us the tools to enable us to live it in our own generation. It is this tradition that has fired us with the spark that makes us long to carry the story further, to make it known to others, and to deepen our own understanding and appreciation of its treasure.

If "tradition" represents a particular faith or denomination for you, bring to mind everything that this means for you. The shape and function of your boat will have been significantly shaped by this tradition. What do you especially value in it? Where, if at all, has it served you less well, and perhaps introduced a few kinks here and there into your boat?

If you come from a home where no one practiced any form of faith or spoke of spiritual matters, everything in the Christian boatyard will seem utterly foreign, and Christians you meet will seem to share a secret language that means nothing to you, maybe leaving you with the feeling that you have to patch a boat together from almost nothing. Don't let that put you off: some of the most seaworthy craft in history have been built exactly like that! This is your boat, and your soul's journey. Let it be whatever it is, and rejoice in it, without trying to conform it to someone else's blueprint about how boats should look.

And if, like me, you are something of a Liquorice Allsort—of dubious spiritual origin and uncertain destination—look at the (possibly) many churches or faiths and traditions that have added a pinch of their own special qualities into your life and rejoice. Remember: no two boats are identical, and all are equally welcome to sail God's seas. Everyone who goes to sea knows both the power and the beauty of the ocean and stands in awe of its mystery. The same is true for all who venture upon a spiritual path, whether or not they can name the ocean of mystery upon which they embark, or identify a particular boatyard as their home base.

Yet there is tension in our relationship with tradition, whatever shape it takes for us. We may be rooted in it, yet we also know the constant desire to move beyond it into uncharted waters. The boat is the product of the boatyard and the particular craftsmen who made it, yet it is made to sail. We acknowledge, wholeheartedly, our indebtedness to all that has shaped us: family, friends, history, culture, and spiritual tradition. And we honor that gifting best when we use it to journey on.

A spot of maintenance

Just as boats don't simply happen, likewise they don't remain in good sailing form unless they are properly and lovingly maintained. So what state do you feel your boat is in? That question, of course, could be a green light for the guilt trip that so often seems to be the first recourse for Christians when they stop to think about their journeying. Many of us have overdosed on a sense of sin. Maintenance isn't about standing in the corner of the boatyard waiting for the cane to descend. It is about valuing the treasure our boat represents, and doing what we can to ensure its seaworthiness. The more we learn to love it, the better we will care for it, and the better we care for it, the more joyously it will journey.

So let's focus on the kind of maintenance that acknowledges that the future begins with today (and not with yesterday). What can we do, in real and practical ways, to keep our craft in good shape?

We have already noticed that we are a fusion of body, mind, and spirit. So it might be worth looking at each of those elements in turn, and drawing up a maintenance strategy.

How well do you care for your body? Do you push it to the limits and then wonder why it breaks down? Do you starve it when its shape displeases you, or give it whatever it happens to fancy while you are watching your favorite TV programs each night? Are you quietly poisoning it? Do you expect it to do an eighteen hour shift each day? Do you give it any exercise? Do you take it away for a holiday every so often? Do you ever wonder what it would say to you if you would only listen? Do you treat your car or your cat better than your own body? Do you regard your family doctor as a necessary evil or a helpful ally? If your answers surprise or dismay you, maybe it's time for a little reappraisal.

And what about your mind? Are you feeding it? If so, on what kind of diet? If you are in the habit of making your body sit up till all hours watching TV or surfing the net, then bear in mind that the diet on offer at precisely such hours may not be the most life-giving. Only you can decide this, but it may be worth stepping back and taking a look at what kind of "supper" your mind is getting just before it takes itself off into the unconsciousness of sleep. And are you exercising it? Do you push it just a little bit beyond its comfort zone, perhaps by encouraging it to play with ideas it hasn't encountered before or questions and challenges it might prefer to ignore? Do you give it any playtime—time to have fun and permission not to take itself too seriously? (Your sense of humor is a good indicator here.) Do you allow it the companionship it needs? Most minds enjoy dialogue with other minds—both like and unlike. Don't lock your mind up in solitary confinement.

And your spirit? What feeds the very essence of you? What gives you life? Does your spirit know how to fly, or have you clipped its wings to fit a particular belief system? Do you know how it feels to be soul-starved? How do you guard against this kind of inner hunger? Your spirit is, in its very nature, a relational being. At the deepest heart of our being we are all one, and our spirits know this intuitively. So maintenance may require a look at your relationships. Are they in good order? Are there any cracks or splinters in the important relationships in your life, and if so, how might they be addressed? Perhaps reconciliations with estranged friends or relatives are needed, apologies where we may have hurt someone, the grace to let those who have hurt us approach us for a new beginning. And finally, what about our relationship with all creation? Whatever affects each of us affects all of us. Failure to maintain our own boat will put the entire fleet in jeopardy.

These questions are offered only as a quick checklist of issues that are common to us all. Perhaps they boil down to the key question: "Do you actually care about your boat?" "Do you like you?" Do you look after yourself adequately, giving yourself rest, recreation, fun and laughter, sleep and nourishment, a circle of good friends and a support system? What about taking time out? Taking time to be still with yourself and with God in prayer and meditation? Making time to reflect on where your life is going and how you feel about it? Maybe think about taking more sustained time out in the form of a spiritual retreat? Seeking out the rest points in all the restlessness? These can all be ways of maintaining your boat, and they are habits worth establishing right at the beginning of the adventure of the voyage, and continuing until your boat crosses the final horizon.

The control center

Whatever the shape of your boat, its center of gravity will be in its control center. Here, at the heart of the matter, decisions will be taken and crucial choices made that will determine the nature and progress of the voyage. So it would be wise to locate this control center and learn how to be at home in it.

Perhaps one of the key differences between "believers" and "nonbelievers" (in the broadest sense of the terms) is that "believers" would be aware of a center of gravity in their lives that is located deeper than their own consciousness or will. The center of gravity is envisaged as being not only within themselves, at the core of their personal being, but also "other" than themselves, and mysteriously at one with the heart of all creation. "Nonbelievers" would probably assert that the center of gravity of their lives is ultimately located only in themselves, and that there is no transcendent "Other" beyond that realm.

This book is basically a book for "believers," in this sense, and it therefore assumes that the control center of your boat is the place where you encounter that "Other," whom most of us call "God." It is this assumption that is the beginning of the difference between being merely "at sea," and being "at sea with God."

It is very easily said, of course, that we acknowledge that "God is in control" of our lives. Most of us would not wish to deny it, yet what does it really mean, and how can we make it true in practice? We may salute God as our guide and navigator, but do we ever let God take the helm? We may revere God's wisdom, as revealed in all the maps and charts of sacred scripture and the evidence of God's creation, but do we take it into account when our hands are on the tiller?

A few suggestions might help to turn what we want to do into what we actually do:

- If the control center is at the heart of our voyage, and is the place where the vital choices will be made, surely we need to visit it regularly? This might mean seeking out time and space for personal prayer, meditation, and reflection, not only while making decisions, but regularly. In such time and space, the center of gravity around which we live our normal, everyday, "ego-centered" lives, drops to a deeper level, where it touches the center of gravity of all being. Only in this deeper center will we gradually learn to respond to the tides and currents of our lives in a way that is in harmony with God and all God's creation.

- The listening and discerning that happens in this "center" nourishes and shapes the partnership between each of us and God, and this partnership leads to a deep intuition that increasingly informs our decisions. We don't need to be neurotic about spending all our waking moments in the "control center." If we are developing the habit of spending some time simply being still in this "center," then God will be given the space and freedom to weave life-giving patterns out of every choice we make.

- What does this "center of prayer" mean for you? Do you spend time there regularly? Just a few minutes each day in this "control center" of our hearts will help us to take our bearings for the day. If this isn't a habit in your life, you might like to look at ways of incorporating real and living prayer into your daily life. If you don't know where to begin, some useful resources are listed in the bibliography.

- You can't spend all day cooped up in the control center. God wants you, above all, to enjoy the voyage. In the same way, you can't spend all day in your private prayer corner. The art is to spend time, consciously, each day, checking things out with God, and then trusting that the growing partnership between you will steer the craft on a true course. This certainly doesn't mean abandoning all personal responsibility for the course you are plying. Rather, it means remaining alert and aware yourself of the "signs of the times"—the movements going on in the surrounding waters, the storms that are brewing up in your life, the feelings of being stuck and going nowhere, the hopes and dreams of the destination. All these are matters to bring to the control center and work through with God. This is the art of reflective living, and is the beginning of a continuing dialogue between your (true) self and the transcendent presence of God.

- And finally, what maps and charts are in your control center? What do you find there that will help you to discern, with God, the best course ahead? For most of us these maps, charts, and navigational aids are what have been given to us in the boatyard. They come from our own spiritual tradition. For many, sacred scripture will be the most important of the charts. Many will value the sacraments as vital aids to navigation. Stories and examples from those who have gone before may line the shelves of the control center. The riches of other faiths may also have their part to play in assisting in your voyage. Just take a little time to reflect on what most helps you in your Christian journeying, and to what extent you really use these aids effectively and personally.

Reflect

Not all the charts were delivered ready-made from the boatyard. Other charts are ours alone to discover. What draws us closer to God and what tends to pull us away from our true center, what personal stars guide us forward, what dreams do we follow, and why? These are charts that we discover only in our own hearts. They are about our own sacred story. Have a look at your own "charts," and take a moment to notice their shape and content. Can you give a name to what you most deeply long for? Can you identify what it is that keeps you going on this journey of faith? If God were to sit down beside you right now and ask, "Where would you like us to sail to? What is the most important thing to you?" how would you reply?

A vital piece of equipment on most boats is the radio link back to the outside world, to the coast guards and to other mariners. At sea, on VHF radio, channel 16 is maintained as the emergency/call-up channel and is the channel on which everyone keeps a listening watch. Sailors know that they must keep channel 16 open at all times, whatever they may choose to transmit and receive on any other channel. What about your own "channel 16"—your personal link to God. Is it always open? To keep "channel 16" continually open is to live in the steady and continuous awareness that your center of gravity is not located solely within yourself. It is to live reflectively, knowing that you are not thrashing around in open seas without map and compass, but in a creative partnership with the one who created you. And if your channel 16 is open to God, it will, necessarily, also be open to hear the cries of any other seafarers around you who may be in need.

The control center, of course, is also the place where the compass is located. Using the compass is another story—one that we will explore more fully in a later chapter. For now, let's pass on to the matter of how your boat is fueled.

The fuel supply

Our local fitness center has a hydrotherapy pool. This is a wondrous arrangement that lifts you high on a surge of warm swirling water if you are standing, or sitting, in the right place at the right time. When the water is in motion, it supports you totally and effortlessly. You are carried entirely by an energy other than your own. At other times the water behaves in the usual way of water, simply lapping around you. The geography of the pool seems to be something that seasoned users understand and use to their advantage. They know how the water will behave, and which parts of the pool will become "active" next, and they make sure that they are standing in the optimum position.

Energy surges like this happen in everyday life too. They can appear to be random, but closer observation will reveal certain personal patterns. When the energy is flowing, things move on, and we feel held and supported. When the energy fails, we can feel flat and weary. Over a longer period, we can begin to recognize that certain aspects of our lives provide us with energy, and other aspects drain us of energy.

So what does this reveal about the way your boat is fueled? It might be worth taking another look at the boat you imagined yourself to be. What do you feel is its main source of energy? Perhaps it runs mainly on energy that seems to come from beyond yourself, like a sailing boat catching the wind and skimming the waves? Perhaps you feel you often have to work rather hard at the job yourself, like an oarsman struggling to shift a rowing boat through heavy seas? Maybe you feel the need to fall back on motorized assistance, or even a towrope, by calling on others to help you in the task? Most likely your life draws its energy from all these sources at various times and in different situations and relationships. Sometimes you will feel so energized that the project in hand flows freely and bears rich fruit. Sometimes you will feel that you are struggling in heavy seas, and you have to resort to "oars" that are almost too heavy to move, and the task you are dealing with wears you out and exhausts you. And sometimes you will have to call on your standby sources—your friends and colleagues, your family, or other support lines to pull you through a bad patch.

It can be helpful to notice these patterns. As you become more aware of the aspects of your life and work and relationships that seem to give you energy and life, it becomes possible to use this energy more consciously—to put yourself in the way of it deliberately, just as the seasoned bathers in the hydrotherapy pool know where to go to enjoy the maximum benefit of the changing water power. Often the things that energize you actually give you a surplus of energy, which can help you do the necessary things in life that are not life-giving, but nevertheless need to be done. Part of the task of looking after the boat and helping it to remain afloat and keep moving is to recognize these personal sources of energy in your life and give yourself the time and space to engage in those things. A simple example might be that of parenting, where the projects you undertake with your children, the joys of being alongside them in their development, and the love they bestow on you so freely and abundantly, can provide you with more than enough energy to enable you to keep on doing the ordinary chores of family maintenance, and the crisis management that inevitably challenges us from time to time. A helpful approach is to look for ways to maximize the energy supply by engaging in what is life-giving for you, and to minimize the energy losses by avoiding the things that drain you of life, such as arguments and resentments.

This kind of energy balance is a very delicate and complex business, however. The patterns of what energizes us and what drains us go deeper than just our chosen, and unchosen, activities. Most of us have deep, unconscious strategies for gaining energy, and not all of these strategies are legitimate. Many of them are in fact based on theft! We steal energy from each other, instead of going to the Source. And because human motivation is so complex and devious, we usually don't even realize we are doing it. Imagine a world where, whenever the car runs out of gas, we stop and break into another car's fuel tank and siphon off what we need to keep driving instead of going to the filling station. Unthinkable? And yet this way of proceeding is widespread, and indeed almost universal, when it comes to obtaining, and retaining, the vital energy of our living.

A few examples may help to reveal how we all tend to engage in this very damaging practice, and how, in turn we are all to some degree damaged by it. These are a few classic ways of "stealing energy":

- *Putting other people down*, with the result that the insulter gains a sense of being "up." Putting down comes in all manner of forms, from the most subtle to the most brutal. It is especially effective against children, young people, and those who are already feeling vulnerable without your help. Sarcasm is a classic tool for putting others down. Comments like "What? Did you get your drivers license at the fairground?", hurled at a passing driver, may relieve one person's anger but they aggravate another's. I remember being asked by an impatient teacher once in primary school "Were you vaccinated with a gramophone needle, Margaret?" His putdown about my talkativeness gained him a round of laughter from my classmates, but it left me seriously worried about the state of my medical history.

- *Withholding affirmation.* An effective tool especially in the workplace, this keeps the user "up" by holding everyone else "down." The corollary is the knack of taking credit oneself for the achievement of someone else. Many a promotion (and therefore a personal energy boost) has been gained by these means. Many an evening outing has been spoiled by a thoughtless partner commenting "Surely you're not going to wear that, are you?"

- *Destructive criticism.* This method never fails, whatever the context. The energy boost gained by the critic is frequently short-lived, however, because the technique tends to isolate him or her fairly rapidly. I once caught myself telling my six year old not to be "so childish!" I did stop to ask myself afterward whatever I thought I meant by such a stupid remark, but it was too late to undo the negative message that those careless words communicated.

- *The habit of continual correction.* This can take the form of constantly explaining how the world and all it contains could have been better designed by Mr. Right. The improvements range from the management of world affairs, to the rearrangement of the kitchen shelves to prove that your system is superior. This technique boosts Mr. Right's energy levels by implying that everyone else is inadequate. And it can be done so deceptively, under the cover of an offer of help: an impatient, "For goodness' sake, let me do it" speaks volumes about the relative "worth" of the person offering the help as against the person apparently incompetent to manage without it.

- *Belittling another person's profession or skills.* If you don't quite feel up to putting a person down directly, you can always do so indirectly, by diminishing their chosen line of work. Haven't we heard comments like "You teachers spend half the year on vacation!" This also leaves you the get out clause of "I didn't mean you personally!" if they retaliate. Some professions are especially vulnerable, notably the teaching profession, the medical profession, and those who design computers! The knack here is to project our own bad health, failures, or downright stupidity onto other people. The energy loss to the people who receive the negative projection can become institutionalized and very difficult to eradicate. The same method can be used to belittle whole cultural groups or national identities.

- *Refusal to listen.* A great way of putting someone down is to switch off, visibly, when they are speaking to you. This gives them the impression that they are invisible, and hence extremely unimportant. You, however, must be very important indeed, with far better things to do than listen to someone else. Interrupting someone in midsentence, or blanking out their comments and questions is another way of saying "You don't matter, but I do!"

- *Arguing.* Almost every proposition is amenable to argument and contradiction, if you think about it. If you can turn a conversation into an argument, you will rapidly reduce the energy levels of all the other participants, and while they are embroiled in this exhausting process, you can make off with a cache of their vital energy for yourself. Life becomes a Punch and Judy show for such people, leaving little energy to spare for the joy of simply living.

- *Being churlish.* There is a lovely English word, "curmudgeon," that sums up the final technique in this brief list. The one who practices curmudgeonly behavior on a regular basis can steal the energy not just from a few chosen targets, but from everyone he or she encounters. And so a bright "Good morning, lovely day today" evokes the response, "Hmm, but the weather forecast is dire!" A curmudgeonly travel companion is the one who walks around the ferry counting the lifeboats while you are admiring the magnificent seascape. The quantity of energy gained by this means is questionable, because such thieves tend to get caught up in the general misery themselves, and benefit little from their labors. The effect on the rest of us, however, is dramatic.

These techniques come in thousands of variations, and you will no doubt be able to add plenty of tricks from your own experience. There is literally no end to the ways in which we can diminish each other in order to boost ourselves. And it is amazingly easy to see how other people are using, or have used, these methods against you. Much harder is to recognize the subtle ways in which you yourself are using them against others.

Theft like this always has consequences, and they are never life-giving. It always triggers a reaction. Either we fight back, and the end result is conflict, which drains us even further of vital energy, although there may be occasions when fighting back is a necessary and healthy survival strategy. Or we make up the deficit by going straight out to siphon some fuel from another person's tank. Or we turn inward and feel depressed, because we have unconsciously taken the negativity on board.

So what is the alternative? Two questions present themselves:

1. How do we protect ourselves against fuel thieves?

2. How do we stop ourselves from turning into fuel thieves?

The first question isn't easy to answer, but a simple awareness of what is actually going on may be an excellent starting point. Once I am aware that someone is diminishing me in order to make themselves feel better, I am less likely to take the diminishment personally, and therefore less likely to have the knee-jerk reaction of wanting to fight back. I will be better able to recognize that the problem lies with the other person's self-worth and not with my own. I may even be able to explore more creative ways of boosting other people's sense of their own value, so that they won't need to do so much thieving in the future. It also becomes clear, on reflection, that some people consistently tend to drain us of energy. Some corrective action may be called for if particular relationships are revealing a destructive pattern like this.

The second question invites us to find our own legitimate energy sources, so that there will be less temptation to steal energy from others. I would suggest that there are three excellent ways to gain energy legitimately:

1. The first is to draw on the energy that flows freely and abundantly from things we enjoy doing or people we enjoy being with. These are sources of life that inspire us and enthuse us, and leave us feeling more fully alive after the encounter than we were before. In terms of the seafaring metaphor, these are our floating tankers or filling stations. We know what and who they are, and where they are to be found. They may consist of special hobbies or pastimes or skills that we pursue, or companions with whom we can spend quality time, or even something as simple as a phone call to a friend. I once knew an elderly lady who didn't have much spare cash, and got a bit lonely. On special occasions, instead of a more conventional gift, her daughter would cover the phone bill to allow her to make some much appreciated calls to a circle of her old friends. These conversations were like "tankers" for her. And we ourselves are "tankers" for others in ways we may not fully recognize. We can too easily, perhaps, focus on how to get away from the people or things that drain us, when it would be more profitable to try to spend more time with what energizes us.

2. The second is to draw on the energy of the created world. When I feel drained, or otherwise out of kilter, I can get "first

aid" instantly by walking through the garden and reconnecting with the natural world. It's almost as though the sap that rises through the plants and trees gets through to me too, and the expansiveness of the skies above expands my soul and gives me a fresh perspective. Gardeners and hill walkers will be very familiar with this kind of "filling station." A few minutes at peace in the presence of creation can move me beyond the need to go and siphon off my immediate fuel needs from the resources of my fellow creatures.

3. The third—but actually the most important—way is to make sure we are in touch at a personal level with the Source of all energy, who is God. We all have an oil rig in our hearts, and we can draw constantly from that supply of divine energy and love. We do so when we withdraw into prayer and meditation (whether for just a few minutes or for a sustained period of retreat), and every time we stop to reflect on where and how God is active in all that is happening in our lives. If the thought of "prayer" or "meditation" sounds too heavy, try simply taking a little time out regularly: twenty minutes in your favorite chair, just being still; a ten-minute walk around the parking lot alone during your coffee break at work; a little catch-up time in solitude and peace at the end of the day just to think over the day's joys and sorrows and restore perspective to all that has been going on. Gradually the habit becomes part of who you are, and the rewards, in terms of sustainable energy supplies, may surprise you.

Safety on board

Storms can tip us out of our life's comfort zones from time to time, and long-trusted "securities" can let us down. When you look around the boat that is your life, where do you find the safety nets in the event of disaster? How do you protect yourself against dangers? What is your life jacket? Perhaps you are a "belt-and-braces" person, who tends to overdo the safety measures? Or maybe you are a natural risk taker, who thrives on the occasional adrenaline rush? It might be good, before we move ahead, to reflect on where we find our security amidst the changing conditions of life's seas.

When you board a small craft to head out to sea, one of the first things you will do is don your life jacket. And if you have a dog or cat on board, it too will have its own little life jacket. You put the life jacket on over your ordinary clothes, and it gives you buoyancy. And it's something that is worn easily. After a while you forget you are wearing it. This image might help us to explore what it is in our spiritual journeying that keeps us afloat if we go overboard. It is said that the reason the angels can fly is because they take themselves so lightly! And it's the air in the life jacket that saves you from drowning. What is this weightless, invisible "something" that gives life when everything else is lost?

Reflect

To get in touch with what this means for you, you might like to imagine yourself in an emergency at sea. The boat is sinking and you can't take anything overboard with you. Your life jacket is your only possession. In your imagination, think away the various layers of security you depend on. Peel them off, like the skins of an onion, noticing the different degrees of unreliability they represent. For example, imagine life without:

- *Significant personal relationships*

- *An affordable home*

- *The good opinion of those around you*

- *Financial security*

- *Your general good health*

- *Your independence*

- *Your mobility*

- *Your sight, hearing, or mental faculties*

This exercise isn't meant to depress you, but to help you focus on what it is, at the core of your being, that would keep you afloat when all other securities are lost. From your past experience of sudden, painful loss, where are your lifelines? On a boat there is always something to hold on to — the rail, the mast, the ladder. Indeed, we hear of seafarers in heavy seas actually tying themselves to the mast to avoid being swept overboard. What does the mast mean for you? What do you hold on to when all else fails?

You may find that your lifelines are weightless and invisible. Perhaps they are located in the friendships you have forged over the years, and the ones you love, or the extended communities you feel you belong to. Perhaps the buoyancy that keeps you going has to do with your capacity for experiencing joy in life and the awesome beauty of creation. You have been putting on life jackets like these all through your life, and even when all else fails, they will keep you afloat. Make sure, before you set sail, that these intangible lifelines are sound and strong, even as you remember that they, too, are not going to last forever. If you find that your life's securities tend to be found in achievement, wealth, or status (and these drivers operate in subtle ways on all of us!), then some gentle reappraisal might be called for, regarding what you most deeply value, and where the true bottom line of your security is to be found.

Even the most sturdy boats eventually sail over the horizon, back to the Boatyard in the Sky. The physical, and even the mental, components of our boats are not designed to last forever. Sooner or later our faculties will begin to take their leave of us and eventually that fragile framework of skin and bones will disintegrate. Or unexpected storms may throw us against the rocks, and the things we have depended on may suddenly cease to exist.

A group of medical students were spending some time on the psychiatric ward, dealing with elderly patients suffering from depression. The consultant who was tutoring the students gave them this exercise: "Think of four things that make life worth living for you." The students thought of their replies. Then the consultant said: "Now imagine yourselves aged sixty. How many of your four things are still in place?" There was a subdued silence. The consultant went on: "Now think of yourselves as being eighty. How many of your four things are still there now?" The students had begun to discover for themselves why so many elderly people are depressed. You might like to try this exercise for yourself. If the results disappoint you, take a close look at the four things you valued so much in the first place and see whether these are your final word on where you deepest treasure lies.

But safety on board isn't just about me and my own boat. I also have to take care not to harm anyone else or any other boat. If you stroll around a typical marina, or a fishing harbor, you'll notice that the boats are protected against bumping into each other. Obviously, if the wind gets up in the night, or when you are passing through locks or trying to enter the harbor, there is a high chance of accidental collision with your neighbors, or the harbor walls. In daily life this danger is an ever-present reality. In almost every human interaction there is a risk of treading on other people's toes and causing offence, if not injury.

Yachts have "fenders" to prevent this (fishing boats tend to use old tires—less smart but equally effective), and when I look at the fenders, I can't help feeling we have something to learn from them. They are simply cushions of air, to prevent the possibility of impact by maintaining a safe space between vessels. How do we cushion the spaces between us? An obvious method is to apply the universal rules of civility. A more challenging way of providing spiritual fenders might be to practice the skill of empathy. Putting ourselves deliberately in our neighbors' shoes, and setting aside our own agendas, if only for a short time, can make defensive space between people into creative and therapeutic space, where new ways forward may be discovered. A third kind of fender is what we might call "the ham in the sandwich"—the mother who stands between warring siblings, for example, or the diplomat who genuinely seeks to bring conflicting factions together around the conference table. "Blessed are the peacemakers," said Jesus. Better to be a fender than an offender.

A path across the sea

When I contemplate the fragile, transient nature of our life's voyage, in our Brendan-style currach, or our *Kon-Tiki* raft, I am reminded of a magical night crossing of the Irish Sea. There was a full moon, and the sea was calm. I stood on the deck and gazed at the silver pathway that stretched from just below my feet, right across the seas, to the source of the light. Perhaps other people were gazing at this pathway from the coastline of Ireland, or from the harbor walls at Holyhead in Wales, or indeed from any other chosen place on Earth. Wherever they were, that pathway would always begin at exactly the place they were standing, and stretch across the seas to join them with the source of the light, just as it began at the feet of Brendan, and of the South American adventurers, and of all who have set sail in little boats on incredible journeys. I felt unaccountably close to all these other moon gazers, all these other human "vessels" who, like me, were searching for the pathway across the oceans of life, to the Source of that Life, and to everything that lies beyond the horizons of Mystery.

The pathway begins here, where you are standing right now, and it stretches all the way to God, who is at once the source of the Light, the pathway that leads to it, and your own desire to travel that path.

CHAPTER

The Cargo and the Crew

I couldn't have chosen a more appropriate moment to visit the *Cutty Sark*, a historic tea clipper in dry dock at Greenwich. I had seen her masts so often, soaring above the city skyline, but it happened that, for once, I had both the time and the inclination to go on board, and that, for once, the vessel was almost empty, it being a grim and gale-driven January afternoon. Afterward I pottered around a little shop in Greenwich that specializes in all kinds of nautical bric-a-brac, and there I bought an inexpensive model skiff that appealed to my imagination.

Safely back in the place where I was staying, I took out my new toy for closer inspection. It was just a little replica rowing boat, of the kind that might be used for a fishing trip in the Mediterranean, with a single sail to catch the breeze and ease the effort in the arm muscles when the wind is right. It came complete with a set of little wooden oars, a rudder, a replica baling-out bucket, life-saving ring, an anchor, and a few coiled threads for ropes, and that was it! As I played with it I found myself mentally packing it with all the other things I would probably think I couldn't do without, should I be about to set sail in such a boat.

And as I pondered all the "cargo" I might think of loading onto my little skiff, I remembered the vast holds of the *Cutty Sark* (and every plank still smells of tea!). I recalled the care with which the cargo had been battened down and protected, so that however much the crew suffered under the gales and massive walls of wild water, the tea, at least, would not get wet! And especially I remembered the Plimsoll line painted in white on her hull—the markings that would indicate her loading and warn of overloading before it was too late.

Loading and overloading. Important cargo, essential supplies, unnecessary baggage. How do I tell the difference? My own life's vessel has some major problems with overloading, and not everything I

31

carry in my little skiff is either necessary, or even desirable. How do I begin to sort out what I really need to carry with me through my life, and what is overloading and unbalancing me, to the extent that the warning levels of my spiritual "Plimsoll line" are in danger of disappearing entirely below water?

And the crew? The *Cutty Sark* plied her way back and forth between Europe and China with just twenty-eight men, eight of whom were apprentices. And my little toy skiff probably represents a one- or two-man expedition. What kind of "crew" mans my life's boat? Who sails with me on my life's voyage? What tasks do they represent that I need to attend to as I sail?

These are some of the questions that will guide our thoughts in this chapter.

What are you "taking on board"?

How often have I heard this phrase, or used it when speaking to others? "Have you really taken that on board?" we ask. Or we warn ourselves, "I don't have to take that on board."

There are some things that can actually be rather difficult to take on board. The kind of things we hear spoken to us, or about us, but don't quite manage, or don't quite dare, to believe. Or we might take them in with our heads, but refuse them entry at the deeper levels of ourselves—our heart and our gut.

Here are a few examples of truths that it might be good—even essential—to take on board:

- I am more than a cupful of carbon and a few liters of water.

- I am not an accident.

- I have special gifts to offer and I can rejoice in that giftedness.

- I am worthy of others' love and I am capable of loving others.

- I am not being asked to carry my past with me.

- I can be free of past programming.

- My mistakes and wrongdoings may have been serious, but they were not terminal.

- I do have my faults, and if a friend points them out, it is the faults she is criticizing, not me as a person and a friend.

- Wherever we are going, we begin from today.

- I don't have to allow others to steal my vital energy.

- I don't have to steal their energy: I can get my own from the Source.

- I have a unique voyage to make, and my voyage is uniquely precious in the eyes of God. No one has the right to tell me otherwise.

- I have been given the tools I need to navigate my own course.

- I can trust my own experience.

Reflect

These are all statements that we all have been challenged to take on board at some time or another. As you read through this list, how do you feel about each of these statements? Are there any you can't take on board? Is there anything you would add to the list?

If any of these important personal resources speaks to you especially—either positively or negatively—spend some time with it in quiet reflection. Live with it, and chew on it, until it reveals to you whatever it is trying to tell you.

Most boats have some kind of ballast or keel to keep them in the water, and upright. Truths such as those listed above could be compared to a keel. They stabilize us in our voyaging. They are our personal "bottom line" when it comes to faith. The design of the keel can be important. Too light, or nonexistent, and the vessel will skim at high speed through the water, but may not hold up under stress and will be more difficult to control. Too heavy, and the vessel will sit solidly in the water but may not move very far or very fast. Getting the stabilizing factors right is an important exercise.

Your personal story may not have offered you much in the way of emotional and spiritual stability. You may not have experienced as a child what it means to be loved without having to earn that love in the currency of good behavior or impressive achievements. You may not have enjoyed financial security or a stable home background. As life moved on, you may never have known the joy of a permanent, committed, and loving relationship with a partner or in a community. You may feel, as a result, that your boat doesn't have a keel. Perhaps God compensates the keelless boats by giving them the very real gift of being more responsive to the storms and weather that life can throw up. Long years of practice in dealing with life's disappointments and failures can be a very real gift to take on your future voyage. Such experience can also make you into an especially sensitive companion for others.

On the other hand, your boat's keel may be too heavy for the job, and may even be impeding your journey. Examples of an over-heavy keel might include:

- Suffocating, dependent relationships that prevent you from moving on, perhaps through a misplaced sense of guilt or duty.

- Fears that lock you into a need for "belt-and-braces" security, tempting you to try to protect yourself from everything, from inclement weather to stock market crashes.

- Allegiance to religious practices and obligations that are based on fear rather than on love, that impose control rather than enabling real freedom, or that verge on the superstitious.

Reflect

So, without judgment, just take a look at what it is that stabilizes your boat, and how you feel about it. If it feels that there really is no keel—no real provision of stability in your story—look again at the facts we began with. You can choose, in the here and now, to take these facts on board as you journey on. If you feel your story is overburdened with security, and in danger of becoming land-locked, just take a cool look at what it is that is making you, as it were, "bottom-heavy," and whether you feel ready to free yourself of any of it. As we look more closely, later in this chapter, at some of our unnecessary baggage, you may discover for yourself new ways of doing this.

What cargo are you carrying?

Your boat isn't sailing the high seas of life just by chance. If you believe that the human story is going somewhere, and that the center of gravity around which it moves is located not in personal satisfaction, but in something bigger than that, someone we call God, then you will have a sense of being involved in a larger destiny than that mapped out merely in your own immediate circumstances.

One of the questions that have always engaged the human mind and spirit is embedded in this sense of destiny. If we are part of a story infinitely bigger than our own story, and yet a story into which our individual story is intimately interwoven, what is our personal journey through life really all about? How can we discover what unique thread our story brings to the larger tapestry? In terms of the seafaring metaphor, what unique cargo is our life's boat carrying?

The *Cutty Sark* was a tea clipper. No one who goes aboard her now can remain unaware of the many tons of tea she has carried across the world. Tea is in the very air, and every plank of her decks is steeped in its lingering aroma.

At this point, then, maybe stop to reflect on what unique gift or calling you are carrying through life and who it might be intended for. Jesus called his first disciples, who were fishermen, to become men who would bring their fishing skills into the great task of bringing God's wholeness to planet Earth. He used the language and the image that was closest to their own experience. So what would he be saying to you?

Reflect

What skills do you already have? What are you good at? What do you most enjoy doing? How might these features of who you are be employed more actively for the growing of God's Kingdom?

What experience has your life so far given you? Perhaps you have gathered years of work experience in a particular field. Perhaps you have accumulated experience through caring for others, bringing up children, learning to adjust creatively to the demands imposed by others?

If you had a free choice about how you would spend the rest of your life, what direction would you feel drawn toward? This desire, even if it seems unlikely to be fulfilled, may be suggesting something important about the cargo you are carrying. And as the years unfold, the desire you secretly cherish may well prove to be the direction in which God draws you, in ways that might surprise you.

Draw these reflections together in this little exercise: Imagine that you have been asked to describe yourself in a paragraph. Maybe you are to speak at some function, or open a supermarket, or whatever. The organizers want to know something about you to put on their publicity for the event. The challenge is to tell them, in a nutshell, what you feel the very essence of you is about. You could just give them a superficial view—your qualifications or your age and appearance, for example—but is that the message you want to go out to hundreds of people who will read the flyers about your forthcoming visit? Try to catch a glimpse of your own soul and express it in a few words (or a picture if you prefer).

So this special cargo, that only your vessel can carry, has to do with your personal gifting, your experience, your innermost desires and longings, your sense of what it is that makes you you. For reasons you may never fully understand, it matters supremely to God that you live the fullness of who you are, and carry it faithfully through your life, sharing it generously at all the ports God guides you into along the way. It is a cargo that grows as you give it away, and however much it grows, the vessel of your being will always expand to accommodate it. It will never weigh you down; on the contrary it will give your heart wings. It will be both the energy and the purpose of your voyage.

Another way of looking at your cargo is to see it as a reflection of the kind of creative life and love that Jesus of Nazareth demonstrated in every facet of his own living. He spells out for us, fairly clearly, what kind of cargo we are being asked to carry to the world, and these ideals are reflected in the tenets of most of the world's spiritual traditions. Some obvious examples include:

- food and drink for those who hunger and thirst

- shelter for those who are exposed

- gentle care and a listening presence for those who are hurting

- acts of solidarity with those who are marginalized

- freedom, respect, and the experience of being valued as human beings for those who are struggling in some form of captivity or oppression

- new vision for those whom circumstances have blinkered or rendered blind

- authentic encouragement for those who are teetering on the brink of despair

- an "invitation in" for all who have been excluded, by society, family, or religious system

- anger and action on behalf of those too weak to stand up for themselves

- realistic hope for those who can't find any reason for carrying on

- companionship for those who feel alone in their experience of suffering

These are a few of the things that Jesus carried with him through the world and delivered freely to all who had need of them. Do any of these items of cargo strike a particular chord with you? Which, if any of them, do you feel particularly attuned to? What do you think it may mean to you personally, to "carry the Good News"? For some this may mean active service of some kind, for others unregarded quiet prayer. For some it may mean tackling head-on some of the issues of peace and justice in a broken world; for others the gentle passing on of values to their children and grandchildren. But for all of us, the Gospel values that Jesus embodied are a very important key to discovering what, specifically, our own life's cargo is about.

Our cargo hold—God's recycling plant

Life is a long-haul voyage for most of us. The resources we pack on board when we set out are going to need regular replenishing as we journey. I know that I have my own familiar moorings where I can dock for a while and take on board fresh supplies for the onward journey. They are places and, more importantly, people who give me a special kind of oasis, and renew me with their own particular kind of encouragement and wisdom and nourishment. They are my "home ports." You will have your own, and only you will know who and where they are.

I was wandering around the garden of one of my personal home ports one morning in the very early spring, quite simply letting myself be aware, before God, of how deeply thankful I was for this oasis. Idly I got to thinking that if I were sailing my course, stocking up with supplies at my own refueling ports, but dropping off cargo at my delivery ports, the balance in my hold would become a bit skewed. My "own needs" side would be fully stocked, but my "cargo for others" would be continually diminishing. The boat would become lopsided! These were just idle, pre-breakfast thoughts, and I didn't pay them too much attention. But as I continued my gentle, reflective walk around the garden, it struck me that in practice there is a continuous recycling process going on. The resources we need for ourselves, and that are given in the personal oases that we seek out, actually become the raw material of the cargo we are carrying for others!

The equation is deceptively simple: the unconditional, nonjudgmental love we are given by our friends becomes the love we deliver to others. The wisdom we share around our friends' firesides becomes the vision we can offer to those who are struggling in life's fogs. The freedom we enjoy to be simply who we are when we are in a place we can regard as one of our home ports gets recycled into the ability to liberate and enable others on their journeys.

My cargo hold, it seems, is far from being just some kind of storage space. It is alive with God's own production line, continually transforming all I receive in my day-to-day experience of God's love and ever-presence into the cargo I am charged to carry into God's waiting world.

On the other hand . . .

Not everything we want to stow aboard our little boat is truly part of its cargo. A great deal of it, for most of us, is baggage. And there is a difference!

As I played with my little model skiff, I caught myself already, in imagination, stowing all kinds of "extras" on board. As well as all the food I would need, and the fresh water, or one of those clever machines that desalinates sea water, I would need plenty of notebooks (what would I do for years at sea if I couldn't write?!), which meant a supply of pens, pencils, and pencil sharpeners—well, to be realistic, I guess what I would really need on board would be a computer, a printer, an Internet connection . . . and the stock of books I couldn't possibly live without might just about fit into the cavernous hold of the *Cutty Sark*. And so it goes on.

Life Laundry

But baggage isn't just a bad joke. It can be a key to understanding ourselves, and the imbalances that may exist in our attempts to be in relationship with each other and with Someone bigger than ourselves. BBC television ran a series called *Life Laundry*. It was light entertainment of the type that left you feeling quite unaccountably disturbed. At one level it was just another "makeover" program. It revealed how an individual person, or a household, was "cleansed" of the clutter that had accumulated through the ages, and was enabled to begin again in a much more congenial living space. In practice, however, it led to some real soul-searching, guided by a psychologist who gently, though sometimes very firmly, rooted out not just the mountains of clutter, but the reasons why the clutter had been allowed to accumulate. In some cases the encroachment of so much baggage had seriously damaged personal relationships.

Spiritual clutter can be even more disabling, and at this point, before we set sail, we may need to take a long cool look at what we might be carrying with us that could threaten the stability of the boat and the harmony among the crew. Not to mention the probability that the more baggage we carry with us, the more likely we are to spend so much time arranging it and rearranging it, that we actually miss the experience of the journey.

A good guide, it seems, when deciding what you really need on your life's boat, and what is potentially overloading you and needs to be shed, is this simple rule.

Keep only:

- what you know is useful, or

- what you cherish as beautiful.

The rest can go!

Reflect

I would invite you to use these two simple criteria, as you take a look at some of the spiritual and emotional clutter you may be carrying around with you. Some typical incarnations of this kind of baggage are set out below. They are a band of

*stowaways. Have a close look at these potential offenders
and ask yourself:*

- *Do I recognize this piece of baggage?*

- *If so, is this item useful? Is it leading to life, or is it
  dragging me down?*

- *Is it something that enhances, at the deepest level, my
  own life or the lives of those I love?*

*If you recognize an item of baggage, but it doesn't pass either
of these two tests, can you choose to let it go? Wanting to
let go may not, of course, be at all the same thing as actually
being able to let go, but it is a very good start.*

Dealing with the stowaways

In *Life Laundry*, the presenter arranged for all the unnecessary clutter to be assembled out on the "collector's" lawn, or in another suitably large and fairly public place. The collector was then required to sift through it all and make sensible decisions, using questions much like those above, about what to keep. The rest was either sold, given to charity shops, or scrapped. So, as you ponder the items listed below, if you find any that are lurking in your own life, bring them out and take a good look at them (perhaps with a close friend, if that helps). Maybe make a list of your findings, naming the factors concerned. Then look crucially at why it might be that you are still clinging on to them. Usually the accumulation of excessive clutter is an indicator of some insecurity—a kind of defense barrier against the world or a protection against facing some unfinished business. Hoarders, like squirrels, are trying, unconsciously, to secure themselves against a "winter season." Spiritual and emotional hoarders are perhaps doing something similar. There is something about the objects (or attitudes) that are being clung to that has almost become ingrained. To part from it might feel like losing a limb. Jesus reminds us that it might be better to lose an eye than to pitch one's whole being into inner blindness. Radical separation from our baggage may be the beginning of radical healing.

So let's inspect these potential stowaways who are filling up the boat without paying the fare.

- *Old hurts and resentments.* You know the type of thing: "We're not going to so-and-so's wedding because his parents have slighted us in the past." You may have your own versions of these scenarios. They are very energy-inefficient. We pour enormous amounts of our vital energy down these black holes, and we never seem to get any return on our investment. Letting go isn't easy, but if we don't, we may endanger the boat.

- *Assumptions and prejudices that we have stored away in our minds and hearts.* Do you catch yourself coming out with a pat reaction, for example, when particular topics come up in conversation? Do you regularly ride any hobbyhorses? (You might need a kind friend to help you discern this!)

- *Comfort blankets that we have actually grown out of but can't let go of.* What do you do, and how do you cope, when you come up against opposition, disappointment, or feelings of rejection? Are you happy with your coping mechanism, or does it remind you of nursery tactics? For myself, I can recognize that my standard coping mechanism remains much as it was when I was five—to hide away in a quiet corner and hope that the trouble, whatever it is, will go away.

- *Too much busyness, being concerned about too many things where only one is needful,* as Jesus pointed out to Martha in the Gospel narrative. Is your life clogged up with activity? Do you ever hear people say to you: "I would have phoned, but I know how busy you are!" What is the "busyness" actually about? Is it genuine, or is it a cover for deeper feelings you find it difficult to face—perhaps of loneliness or insecurity and a low self-esteem?

- *The ropes of old programming that stop us leaving the harbor—fears, and old ways of responding to new situations.* I know, for example, that I still respond to current situations instinctively using some of the ways of responding that I learned as a child, even though these responses may be wholly inappropriate to the situations I am facing now. A typical "rope" that holds us firmly in the harbor is the one that says "You could never do that—you're not clever enough!" and so we don't even try. Possible failure is something we don't want to risk. Another killer rope tells a story like this: "If you do such-and-such Mummy and Daddy may be cross with you." This rope can hold us back from confronting things in our environment for fear of provoking the opposition or anger of others. Sometimes these are things that seriously need to be confronted, whatever "Mummy and Daddy" might say (whoever they are for you now in your adult situations).

- *Undue attachments that we dread to lose, or long to be rid of, and therefore focus all our energy on.* When our daughter was very small, we could always tell when she was upset. The number of soft toys in her bed would multiply alarmingly. We would smile about this, and comment on the sudden increase in the "teddy bear count," but of course it was a signal that something needed attention, and I hope we tried to act on that signal. Now, as an adult, I can see that my emotional "teddy bears" have become a kind of baggage that I carry around with me and seek solace in when things go wrong. Sometimes the attachment can be localized to a tendency to graze from the fridge. Sometimes it is a more damaging attachment, such as a dependent need of another person, where the dependency is making real relationship impossible. Do you have any addictive attachments that look at all like this?

- *The machinery of false guilt that traps us in self-focus and puts us at the mercy of manipulative power systems.* False guilt is a malicious stowaway, not least because it often masquerades as something good. We have often accumulated a mountain of false guilt as children, so much so that we are programmed to see potential "sinfulness" in just about everything we think or feel or do, especially if we are enjoying it! And the chief (though often unwitting) sources of such guilt complexes are loving parents who mean well, efficient teachers who try to educate well, and righteous religious systems that aim for our "salvation." If you recognize the traces of such false guilt around your story, just take a look at where it is coming from, and whether you still want to give it house-room.

- *Poor self-image that convinces us that our own voyage doesn't matter.* As a result, we are very quick to drop our own cargo, and abandon our own dreams, usually to pick up someone else's, because we have an ingrained belief that our own story is insignificant and everyone else's story is very important indeed. Poor self-image makes us into submissive (and often resentful) servants, compliant partners, and excellent doormats. If this stowaway is lurking in your boat, you are in danger of getting sucked into other people's journeys. Your boat is likely to be in tow to another, apparently stronger, story. You may even discover that your whole life is devoted to the living out of someone else's dream.

- *The victim mind-set.* This stowaway will probably be looking a bit droopy, because he has chosen to live his life assuming that, since he once suffered some undeserved harm, every new situation is also going to prove harmful. He has incorporated the perception of himself as a victim right into his sense of identity. "Victim" has become part of who he feels he is, and parting with that aspect of his assumed identity can feel like losing a vital organ. This kind of baggage appears in many guises. For example: I overtake a slow driver on the motorway, but as I try to pass him, he seems to accelerate. If I am carrying a victim mind-set around with me, I immediately assume malice aforethought: the offending driver is deliberately trying to annoy me. In fact most other drivers are concentrating almost solely on making life difficult for me!

- *Other people's baggage.* This is the catch-all, for anyone who doesn't have any baggage of their own! What are you carrying that is not actually yours to carry? Are you taking responsibility for another person's journey (and actually preventing them from making it themselves)? Are you permitting other people to load their concerns onto your shoulders in a way that goes beyond normal human compassion and a readiness to help with life's burdens? When someone else in the family gets into a scrape, do you feel guilty? When there is bad feeling in the office, do you accept responsibility, so as to get the atmosphere breathable again? When your perfectly adult friend makes a bad decision, with bad consequences, do you lie awake worrying about what you could or should have said or done to prevent the problem? These are just a few clues that may indicate that your baggage is not all your own.

One way in which we human beings frequently deal with our unwanted baggage is to project it onto someone else. We find ourselves thinking that if only such-and-such were not around in our lives, everything would be fine. I remember once hearing about a young woman who entered an enclosed religious order after graduating from university. She wrote back to her former friends, and, among other things, commented that the so-called "recreation hour" was the worst part of the day. The sisters were supposed to sit together and be nice to each other, but, as she admitted, she often found herself thinking that if only Sister X were out of it, the circle would be more tolerable. In her imagination she would think Sister X away, only to discover that Sister Y then became the focus of her irritation. And so it went on, until she was the only one left in the room. At which point it became painfully obvious where the real source of the problems lay! You might like to try this exercise (silently of course!) on your own circle of colleagues, friends, or family, "getting rid" of each one who "offends" you, until only you are left. Where is the baggage now?

Of course, it isn't at all easy to jettison this unwanted baggage. No amount of persuasion or coercion will do the trick. But what can make us willing to part with these things is the desire to move on in greater freedom. When our desire to sail free is stronger than our attachment to the baggage, then, and only then, we will let it go. A story came my way of an Albanian refugee, who, with her two infant children, was fleeing from terrible violence that most of us could not begin to imagine. She managed to board a boat sailing for Italy, clutching her children, a change of clothes, a bag of diapers for the baby, and her pocket Bible. When the boat was underway, it became apparent that it was seriously overloaded, and the crew came around, insisting that the passengers throw all their baggage overboard. When they reached the Albanian woman, one of the sailors took hold of the baby, and another took her meager bag of belongings. "Either you let your luggage go," they told her, "or the baby goes overboard." That is the kind of choice that focuses the mind and heart, and clarifies beyond doubt what we really desire. Once that clarity is reached, it becomes much easier to loosen our grip on everything that is less than essential.

The crew

We have established the need for our own resources, as we make this voyage through life, we have reflected on the nature of our own unique cargo, and we have looked at some of the excess baggage we may be carrying with us. Before we move on, however, we might pause to reflect on who is with us in this boat we call our life. Who are our personal "crew," and how do we feel about them?

Of course, you may feel that yours is a "one-man boat," and you can proceed best if you have no interference from any other quarter. For a very few of us this may possibly be true, but I would dare to suggest that the vast majority of us would be very ill advised to set sail entirely devoid of other human companionship.

So who do you feel are your close companions on your voyage? And what is it, particularly, that you value them for? How well do you work together, and is there anything you would like to change in the arrangements?

A brief look at the crew of the *Cutty Sark* may possibly open up a few lines of thought. We learn, from the records, that a typical crew of such a vessel might have included:

- The captain (of course!)

- A small and select team of experienced mariners

- The cook (very important!)

- The ship's carpenter

- A few "ordinary" seamen

- Some apprentices

This lineup suggests the most important aspects of the work going on board a working boat like the one our lives represent. For example:

- The role of navigator / co-navigator, someone alongside us who shares the voyage at an intimate level, encouraging us in our discernment of where our lives are going and what vision, or hazards, may lie ahead. For many, this person would be a "soul friend" or spiritual companion with whom we regularly share our experience of what seems to be going on in our spiritual journeying.

- A "faith community" of some kind. This may take a traditional form of "church," or it may be a less formal arrangement. Such a community sets our own faith journeying in the context of a larger wholeness—the whole family of God, however we envision it. All of us can find ourselves floundering at times, in seas that are too deep or too stormy. And all of us experience the better times, when the passage seems smoother. In our personal community of fellow voyagers, we support each other in whatever ways are needed, sharing our own experience for the benefit of all.

- Whatever happens on board ship, the cook makes sure that all the crew receive wholesome nourishment. This is the source of their strength for the journey, so the cook has to be kept sweet. Perhaps you've heard about the captain who reproached his crew for criticizing the ship's cook? "Who called the cook an incompetent idiot?" he demanded to know. To which the second mate replied: "Who called the incompetent idiot a cook?" Hopefully your ship's cook can do better than that! Who provides the spiritual nourishment that keeps you going? Sadly many Christians today report that they are struggling to find spiritual nourishment of this kind. Often they are expending a lot of energy in their own ministries, but are not really being "fed" themselves. If this is a problem you can relate to, is there anything you can do about it? It may be worth bearing in mind that spiritual food is often found in unexpected places. What, for example, is feeding you in your everyday lived experience?

Try looking back at the end of the day, just to notice those moments or encounters that made you come alive, and renewed your energy. Is there anything you can do to foster these sources of nourishment? Is there anything you can do to help provide nourishment for others who may also be feeling spiritually hungry?

- The ship's carpenter reminds us that the ship's maintenance needs will always be an issue. Where do you turn when things "fall apart," or when the timbers of your life start to show gaps and splinters? Who bales you out, if the ship starts to take on water? Perhaps this will be a soul friend. Perhaps it will be someone who has no awareness of your spiritual dimension, but reminds you in timely and important ways to look after yourself: someone who takes you away from your desk and encourages you to relax and enjoy yourself sometimes; someone who makes you sit down and take stock; someone who gives you "permission" to say "No!" on occasion. Be kind to your "carpenters," and take heed of their wisdom.

- And finally, the apprentices. When I learned that the *Cutty Sark*, with such a small crew, also carried apprentices on board, it reminded me that we are not just sailing God's seas for our own benefit. We are also carrying the sacred story through the unfolding pages of our own life experience. We are passing it on, in our own life and times, to those who come after us. You might like to think about your personal "apprentices." Is there anyone to whom you feel called to pass on the sacred story of the unfolding relationship between God and God's creation? Is there anyone who is ready and waiting to learn from you and your skills and life experience?

One group of fellow-voyagers who were not present on board the *Cutty Sark*, but will almost certainly step aboard our own boats from time to time, are those we might call "short-term passengers." There will be many people with whom we have brief encounters—some of them joyous and life-giving, so of them less so. You might like to reflect on some of the people whose lives have briefly traveled alongside your own. Passing encounters can have long-term effects on us, just as we can affect the lives of others quite profoundly, even by something as simple as a chance remark at a party.

On a lighter note, I must add that I have one more indispensable crew member aboard my own boat—the ship's cat! As I write, he is sprawled all over my bed, where he spends most of his life. He is a completely useless object and a total waste of space, and I love him to bits. Of course, at sea the ship's cat is supposed to catch the rats. Mine is too dozy to catch a cold, but God made him and God loves him anyway. You may not have an actual cat in your life, but I do hope there is part of your experience that is likewise wholly unproductive and utterly priceless. Whatever it is, enjoy it, and let it remind you of the importance of simply doing nothing from time to time!

The price of freedom

Before we move on to the challenge of setting sail, we might, in our imagination and our prayer, join a young man who is also hovering around the quayside, deeply attracted by the words and presence of a wise teacher who has recently come on the scene and is drawing great crowds of people, all bringing their own agendas, their needs, their fears, their deepest desires. This imaginative reconstruction is based on the narrative in Mark 10:17–27. Engage with it in whatever way feels right for you.

The wise teacher was about to set off to journey to another part of the country. A traveling healer and itinerant preacher, he was always on the way to somewhere else, and once again it was time to move on.

He traveled light. It was the only way. He embodied the wisdom of the one who once remarked that "we are most rich in what we lack!" Looking into this man's eyes, you could really see the truth of that enigmatic comment. He seemed to carry nothing with him, yet there was something in his gaze that suggested he had everything, and when he looked at you, you knew that, above all, you wanted whatever it was that he had.

Perhaps these were the thoughts that galvanized the rich young man into an uncharacteristic act. Impetuously, he threw himself at the feet of the young teacher, trying, rather unsuccessfully, to put into words what his heart was yearning for.

"Good teacher," he said, "please tell me what I have to do to gain eternal life!"

For a moment the teacher paused in his preparations and looked deeply into the young lad's eyes. This was someone who, in material terms, had everything, he thought to himself, but when you looked closely, you could see that deep inside there was a great empty space. What did he think he meant by "gaining eternal life," the teacher wondered? Was he perhaps looking for that mysterious something that would fill the void inside? Was he trying to express his intuition that there was something more? More to life than being successful or popular, or even merely obedient to the moral codes? More than he could possibly achieve on his own? More than "the world" alone could ever give him?

The textbook reply was easy to deliver:

"You know the rules. Keep the commandments. Deal with others as you would want them to deal with you. Do the things you know belong to being a decent human being. Practice the faith that has been handed down to you."

The young man looked a touch disappointed.

"Master," he protested. "I've been doing these things all my life. I've been trying my best. I live the way the system tells me I should, but I can't get rid of this feeling that there is something hugely important that I am completely missing. It's as though I'm safely moored here in the harbor, doing all the right things, but my boat is actually longing to set sail and discover something more deep, more true—something "eternal." And you seem to have it, whatever it is. Please tell me the secret."

By now the teacher's gaze was penetrating right to the heart of the young man. His eyes became deeply serious. This man's hunger was reaching for more sustaining nourishment. He was ready—perhaps?—to journey into deeper water.

"Yes," he replied, after a few moments of silence. "You are right. There is more. Your heart wants to journey further. But the way is narrow, like passing through the eye of a needle, and you can only travel there if you are

51

willing to leave all your baggage here behind you. Let go of it all, and journey on with me. I'll take you to where you are longing to be. But for this to happen, you would need to step on board the little boat we will use, and this little boat has no space for any baggage."

The young man closed his eyes and thought deeply. His life's "baggage" passed in front of his inner eyes, like so much luggage revolving around an airport carousel. He could see it all there, packed and labeled: security, popularity, achievements, predictability, comfort, like-minded company, future prospects. The carousel revolved relentlessly, and he wanted to pick off the luggage and claim it safely back. The wise teacher watched, as the young man's face fell, and he stepped back from the brink of deeper commitment. He gazed at him with deep love. One day he would be ready to set sail for deeper waters. But not yet.

How do you feel about this incident? How does the story continue for you? You might feel drawn to have a conversation with the wise teacher and explore, with him, all you are feeling.

CHAPTER

3

Setting Sail

The word "launch" conjures up images of celebration and well-wishing. Perhaps it has suffered somewhat from overuse. I remember very well how, when I worked in the computer industry, we would celebrate the launch of a new product. There would be champagne receptions for the company directors, the heads of the development teams, and some of the more important customers. And there would be press releases and publicity campaigns. There might even be a round at the local pub for the people who had actually done the work! And it was always a tense time. Would the new product sink or swim? A lot could depend on the outcome.

More recently I have enjoyed the experience of book launches. While not quite running at industrial levels of magnificence, they too are celebrations, gathering together the publishers, the editors, the author, and some of the hoped-for readers.

Every launch feels like a beginning. Actually, of course, it is the end of the beginning. It comes after a long period of hard work and a lot of waiting and painstaking preparation. When that bottle of champagne is smashed across the bow of the new vessel, the shipbuilders look back over a job well done and prepare to begin the next project.

So what of our life's little barque? How did it ever get launched? What caused us to set sail on this spiritual quest at all? And what kind of preparation was going on quietly in the background before we ever reached that stage in our journey?

Preparing to put to sea

When I look back over the significant "launches" in my own life, what strikes me most forcibly is that they came as the culmination of long years of preparation. So, for example, being launched into a new job happens after years of training, followed, probably, by a string of failed applications. A book launch is the result of long months in front of a computer screen, composing the text, waiting for inspiration, and maybe fielding a steady stream of rejection slips. A launch, it seems, is often the fruit of years of slow growth and carefully garnered and processed experience.

We noticed in an earlier chapter that our life's "boats" are the product of hundreds of generations of experience in the art of boatbuilding. They are also the result of many years of our personal growth and development. If we are really to understand what it might mean to let our lives be launched upon a more searching spiritual quest for God and for the deeper fulfillment of our Christian vision, we would do well to look, at least briefly, at what this preparation time has been about, and how we manage the tension between everything that leads up to our "launch" and the stages of life that follow in its wake.

How many of us look back over the years that have gone, and regret what we perceive as "a waste of time" in what we have been doing with our lives? I know that I have often regretted not choosing a career path that was more obviously beneficial to the human community. Like many others, I spent years of my life doing a job that was probably perfectly dispensable. With hindsight I might have chosen something that made a more positive contribution to humankind in some direct way, like medicine or teaching (not that I would ever have been competent to do either of those things). But I didn't, and now I am stuck with the memories of what might have been. Not a very fruitful place to get stuck. What moves me on from this place of regret is the dawning realization that through all those years of muddling along in a job that wasn't going anywhere very obvious, I was actually learning skills that are only just becoming useful and directed. I was a technical author, charged with "translating" designer's specifications into a language that the end users of our equipment would find helpful. Now, to my own great surprise, I find myself going through a similar process with some of the obscurities in which the human journey with God has become encrusted. The skills I had to acquire in my days in industry turn out to be a great deal more relevant than I could ever have dreamed.

It is often said that "in God's economy there is no wastage." In other words, whatever happens in our lives, however neutral or even negative it may appear to us, God can, with our cooperation, weave something potentially life-giving out of it. This can sometimes be very hard to believe, especially for those who have suffered serious abuse or betrayal in their lives, yet some of our finest literature and drama and our most enduring folk wisdom draws its inspiration from this very process, and from people who have faced the worst, and lived lives that demonstrate the best, of human nature.

Reflect

Holding this truth and promise in your mind, you might like to reflect back over your own years of experience both at work and at home, in sickness and health, need or plenty, sorrow or joy. With hindsight, can you see any ways in which this wealth of experience has been preparing you to carry your particular skills and abilities into a wider context?

It is said that by far the most dramatic part of a baby's development happens before birth, when this new, unborn creature is still very much in the "boatyard" of its existence. It can seem as though we spend most of our lives in that kind of boatyard. But then something happens. Perhaps the tide suddenly changes. Perhaps the moment is exactly right. Or perhaps we are pushed out of our boatyard moorings as a result of some unwanted trauma. Whatever precipitates the movement, we find ourselves on the slipway, and a very different phase of our journey is beginning. And these watersheds can, of course, recur over and over in our story. Most of us will be able to look back on more than one occasion when God has appeared to launch us into some new depths of God's ocean.

At the turn of the tide

Victor Hugo is quoted as asserting that "no army in the world is as powerful as an idea whose time has come." The great movements forward in the human story have often been associated with an idea whose time has come, and our own spiritual journeying may reveal the same kind of pattern. For some reason that we cannot fathom, something begins stirring within us and we have to respond in some way. God is nudging us along the quayside, and we can almost glimpse the champagne bottle hidden in his back pocket.

What have your own "launches" been like? What shape have they taken and how do you feel about them now, in hindsight?

When I look back over my own story, I notice three patterns of events that have led to some significant "movement" within me.

- There have been times that I might describe as the "full tide experience." These have been moments when I felt something was almost brimming over, and the overflow had to go somewhere. Perhaps the overflow is about some intense curiosity to discover what lies around the next corner, or the sense that there is more—much more—to be discovered, if we can risk stepping across the threshold that lies before us.

- By contrast, crucial movement has often happened in me because of an "ebb tide experience." Sometimes this has been the sense of being drained, or unnourished or otherwise seriously dissatisfied with things as they are. Sometimes it has been worse than that—almost as though the harbor itself were on fire, and desperation made me flee to God in my need, even though that meant flinging myself into unknown waters.

- And thirdly, though less visibly, some of the important movements in my soul have been evolutionary rather than revolutionary, rather like a river deepening until, almost imperceptibly, it becomes an estuary, and then flows out into the open sea.

Most of us will find reflections of these kinds of launch in our own life story. They are also there in the story of the whole human family in its voyaging through history.

The fifteenth century, especially, was a time of full tide, when the desire to explore and discover reached a new watershed. All over Europe an idea was coming to its time. Three streams were converging. The first was a technical stream. Ocean-going ships were becoming a practical reality. The second stream was a fresh understanding of the shape of the world. The fact that the earth is a globe and not a table-top was sinking into people's consciousness. And the third stream to flow into this watershed was the overwhelming desire to discover what lay beyond the horizon. And so, Vasco da Gama opened up the route from Portugal to the Orient. Christopher Columbus pioneered the passage from Europe to the Americas and the West Indies in the vessel *Santa Maria*. John Cabot sailed from England to Canada. Bartolomeu Dias opened the spice route by rounding the Cape of Good Hope in South Africa. And the voyages of Magellan led to the first circumnavigation of the world.

All this activity at sea sprang from a common desire to go further than the eye could currently see or the mind comprehend. Its result was to open up new territory and new possibilities for growth, and to expand the human consciousness exponentially.

Reflect

When has there been full tide like this in your own story? What streams of experience flowed into it? Did you set sail on that high tide of your experience? Do you have a Santa Maria *in your story anywhere? Where did it lead you? What was opened up for you as a result?*

Not every setting sail is a matter for rejoicing, however. If we move on in history to 1620, we find the pilgrim fathers gathered in somber mood on Plymouth Harbor, driven by persecution and fleeing from religious strife to seek new lands. Imagine them embarking on the *Mayflower*, which was to bring them, two months later, to Cape Cod, the beginning of a whole new phase of life for themselves and a new chapter of history for the land they colonized.

More tragically, and shamefully, we might move on to 1847. The people of Ireland are experiencing a low watermark of monumental proportions. The tide has gone out dramatically, leaving an entire population stranded on the beach of famine and consequent disease and death. The people perish in their thousands while the food that their land is still yielding is exported under their noses. Out of the famine come the evictions and the enforced emigrations that cast such a shameful shadow over the history of these islands. Driven by desperation, hundreds of thousands of starving people board the notorious "coffin ships" to make the passage to Canada.

In his powerful book *Famine Diary*, Gerald Keegan described the realities of the emigrations:

> The emigration scheme, though fraudulent and treacherous, is serving one useful purpose. It is raising a flicker of hope in the hearts of many who would otherwise give up. Countless thousands are now ready to take the chance. In fact there will be a veritable tidal wave of departures. (p. 49)

The flicker of hope was fragile. Thousands died en route to "the promised land" and thousands more in the fever sheds where they were quarantined on arrival. We might, in thought and prayer, join a few hundred of them for a brief moment, still fanning the flicker of hope, as they gather on the Dublin quayside, waiting to board the *Naparima*, "an ancient tub of a vessel that has reached a ripe old age." We might respectfully observe the poignant moments as "the hills of Kerry faded out of sight. Tearfully and silently we returned to our cabin." There followed two months in what Keegan describes as "a floating charnel house," on a diet of ship's biscuits and foul water, where burials at sea became the narrative of every day.

Today, the ubiquitous presence of indomitable Irish vitality has become a major component of life in the New World. But for those who set sail from Dublin aboard the *Naparima* at daybreak on 9 April 1847, and on so many similar vessels during that apparently God-abandoned year, the setting sail was an act of desperation.

Reflect

While our personal periods of darkness bear no comparison
with the persecutions that drove the pilgrim fathers to sea, or

atrocity on the scale of the forced emigrations, nevertheless, some of our own times of setting sail may have happened as a result of sheer despair. Do you have any memories of this kind, when circumstances drove you to move on in ways you would not have considered doing in happier times? Are there any Mayflowers *or* Naparimas *in your story? Where did they take you, and how do you feel about the experience now with the benefit of hindsight? In what ways have these enforced launches become springboards for spiritual growth?*

But not every launch in our lives is as dramatic as the setting sail of ships like the *Santa Maria*, the *Mayflower,* or the *Naparima*. Sometimes our living simply moves gently and uneventfully from river to sea. We begin to notice that the relatively safe and confined banks of our river life are widening into something bigger and less predictable. Spiritually, we feel, perhaps, less contained. We are no longer so sure that we have got it all together. The horizons are widening, and our souls seem to be spreading their wings for a more adventurous flight. We understood the ways of the river, but we are beginning to feel deeper currents and a challenge to learn new ways of finding our way in deeper, wider waters. Do you recognize anything of this kind of landscape in your own story?

Pushing off

Leaving harbor can be both joyful and painful. If we are sailing on a full tide experience, the feelings may well be of overwhelming delight and anticipation. If the launch is happening out of an experience of despair or trauma of some kind, then our feelings may be very apprehensive. If our river is simply becoming an estuary, we may hardly notice the moment when we actually set sail.

Frequently, however, the beginnings of new stages of our spiritual growth are marked by a need to push away from the harbor walls of all that we have known this far. Sometimes we push away with the force of anger and rejection. Maybe the harbor has been stifling us and something inside us wants to kick it away. Sometimes we push away with reluctance, knowing that we have to do it but not quite wanting to appear to be rejecting something we cherish, and not too sure how we feel about the unknown tomorrow.

The pushing away is something all of us have done in our earlier lives, when we left the safe haven of our parental home and the securities of childhood to make our own way in life. Some of us will also have discovered how it feels when our children push away from us to set sail upon their own course. At times when I have been in this situation myself, I have found it helpful to remember that the kicks of adolescent rebellion are not a personal assault on me as a parent, but are simply what the adolescent has to do to push the boat out into deeper waters. The kicks still hurt, but I don't take them personally, and I know why they have to happen. Something similar seems to go on when our spiritual lives are preparing to set sail into a new phase of our growth in God.

There may be ropes that are holding us moored in the harbor, and are making the launch difficult. These ropes can take many forms, including, for example:

- The need for security, fear of the unknown, and a reluctance to take risks.

- The fear of offending those we perceive to be the custodians of the harbor.

- The inner laziness that would quite simply prefer a quiet life in a safe haven.

It can also help to remember that the ropes that hold us bound to the harbor may in the future become the ropes that will reconnect us, in appropriate ways, to the many other harbors we will visit in our travels. So let's not be too hard on the ropes. They are not just something to be got rid off. They are to be loosened and hauled on board, and used, in a transformed kind of way, to help us reconnect with others. Thus, the person who knows the pull of insecurity will be better able to connect with the many others who are standing hesitantly on the quayside. The one who has overcome natural indolence will be in a stronger position to encourage others to overcome theirs.

Reflect

Do you feel the tug of any ropes that are preventing you from setting sail? Do you know what they are about? Do you really want to cut free of them? If so, is there any way you can see of helping yourself to do so?

Or is your launch perhaps even more painful than this? Sometimes I feel as though my own life's boat has been standing in dry dock for years on end, being prepared for launching, but I have become so used to my place in dry dock that I don't really want to be anywhere else. Then along come the shipbuilders, and one by one they knock away the props that have been keeping me upright so far. It feels like the demolition of all my securities. Perhaps a nagging question keeps haunting me, about what I really believe, and whether it entirely matches up with the "answer books." When I let one question in, it can feel as though I am opening the floodgates, and everything is up for debate. So, for example, I might ask myself the searching question:

"Why do I still believe? Why am I actually a Christian?"

- Is it because "the church" says I should?

- Is it because sacred scripture provides unquestionable facts?

I can test out these answers, ironically, by thinking them away.

- Suppose, for example, that "the church" in its visible, institutional form, were to disappear off the scene. Would I stop believing?

- Suppose, less credibly, that sacred scripture were to be somehow discredited. Would that make me stop believing?

When I think along these lines, I have to answer "No" to these two questions, and I discover that my believing doesn't depend on either of these two things. There must be something deeper than either of them that keeps me with it. And that "deeper" thing turns out to be something as ephemeral and intangible, yet as life-giving and trustworthy, as the air I breathe—it is my own lived experience of moments when God has touched my life in some way that has made a difference to everything that came after. We all have that experience, however fleeting and occasional, of being in some form and at some time touched by God, or, as D. H. Lawrence describes it, of being "dipped in God." This is the one thing that no one else can ever invalidate or dispute. We know what we know. This is the solid ground of our believing. Even when our everyday experience is dire, and we are clinging to the raft of faith as our only remaining lifeline, we can reconnect to these memories of when God has touched us, probably through the agency of other people, and know that this is really what it is all about—a heart-knowledge that God is real for us, a knowledge that lies deeper than custom or doctrine.

Back to the shipyard, this kind of questioning is what I compare to the knocking away of the props. It can feel as though there is no solid ground any more that we can absolutely trust. What one denomination teaches may be anathema to another. What one generation of Christians propose as unquestionable is overturned by the next. But does our believing depend on these temporary certainties? The ship in dry dock certainly needs the props to support it while it is being built, but once it is launched, the props would become an encumbrance. They have served their purpose, and all that is needed now is the wide ocean of God's love—the lived experience of God's all-embracing power to uphold us and guide us. But this doesn't mean that it is easy to let the props be knocked away. Pushing off is hard and painful work.

A change of management

Something very significant happens when we are launched, whatever form that launching may take. Though we usually don't realize it at the time, we actually move into a new management system. So far we have been under the authority, and subject to the disciplines, of the boatyard. Usually, in terms of our spiritual formation, this will have been simply the way things are done in our faith tradition. Our Christian observance may have been jogging along on a kind of plateau. We may have been going to church regularly and praying in our own way, possibly fairly formally and verbally. Or we may have been simply trying to live by the moral precepts of Christianity, whether or not we feel we belong to any branch of the institutional church.

This plateau of believing may well have been our spiritual home for many years. But then something shifts. Like the young searcher in the meditation at the end of chapter 2, we may become aware of a sense that there is more. We are on the slipway, and the old scene is giving way to a new phase of our Christian discipleship—a new way that as yet we can't begin to understand.

For some people, this kind of spiritual shift is accompanied by profound upheaval in their relationship with the boatyard. It no longer seems to work simply to apply the land rules when we are embarking upon a sea voyage. The disciplines of our journeying take on a different shape. It is no longer sufficient merely to keep the rules that someone else has made, and that are intended to regulate the running of the boatyard—rules about the way doctrine is expressed and handed down, for example, or about the way liturgy is celebrated, or about who is legitimately "in communion" with a particular tradition, and who is not. Suddenly, or gradually, these rules and procedures seem to diminish in importance, receding further and further into a harbor we feel we have now left behind. Yet we still, on the whole, revere that harbor and respect its ways of regulating itself. We acknowledge our indebtedness for all it has given us, and hope to make our own contribution to its work in the future. But right now we are at sea, and very different questions begin to shape themselves and take center stage; questions such as:

- Where are we going, and why?

- How do we find our way in this new uncharted seascape?

- How do we know whether we are on course?

- How do we find companionship and authentic relationship with other seafarers?

- How do we deal with the storms at sea, or keep going through the times when we feel we are helplessly adrift?

- How can we respond to the joy of being at sea, to the motion, the challenge, and the beauty of the voyage across the oceans of our living?

- Where can we drop anchor, and when must we move on?

These are the "ocean disciplines," and they seem to bear little resemblance to the rules that we lived by when we were still on shore. The rule books of the boatyard, while they may well be true and sound, don't seem to give us much help out here on the ocean. In fact it often appears that those who continue to man the boatyard feel threatened by the questions that arise when the boats they have built actually put to sea. There is sometimes an undercurrent, almost of reproach, that it would be altogether more satisfactory if the boats settled down peacefully in permanent moorings, and stopped raising difficult questions about what the voyage is all about. Yet for those who find themselves at sea, these questions simply won't go away, and there is a strong suspicion that we are going to have to discover our own answers.

Anthony de Mello tells a story of a young boy who was a very gifted mathematician. His teacher recognized this giftedness, but the boy would not apply himself to his homework. Instead, he would crib the answers from the back of the book each morning on the bus traveling to school. Eventually the teacher drew him to one side, and told him simply this: "You will never become a true mathematician just by taking the answers from the back of the book, even though, ironically, those answers will usually be right."

The boatyard provides us with answer books, but we will never learn to sail simply by consulting these answer books. We learn to sail by putting out to sea and working out the answers for ourselves. Most of the rest of this book will explore some ways of taking these questions into our living, and allowing whatever answers we discover to guide our onward journey.

A new kind of map

I am a fairly frequent traveler across the North Sea and the Irish Sea, and when I board the ferries I am always fascinated by the ocean charts. Like most passengers, perhaps, I begin by looking for where we are and where we are going, but the charts don't readily provide the kind of information we expect from a land map. Instead they reveal the nature of the ocean we are crossing—its depths and shallows, its hazards and safe channels, its permitted shipping routes.

Suddenly the map isn't green and brown, with hills and valleys, towns and villages, roads and railways. It is forty shades of blue! It doesn't even reveal a recognizable coastline. If the land is suggested at all, it appears on the margins, and we can no longer find our bearings from the old familiar landmarks. The terra firma of our normal expectations has disappeared. The chart looks incomprehensible! My instinct, when I see these nautical charts, is to leave it to the experts and hope they will deliver us safely to the other side.

Do these words ring any familiar bells in our experience of our spiritual journey? Do we take one look at the chart of our inner world and shrink back into the conclusion that this journey must likewise be left to the experts (the theologians, the clergy, or whoever else we regard as "expert"), trusting them to deliver us safely to heaven?

It would be an understandable reaction. However, the journey we are about to embark upon really doesn't give us this kind of option. We are the boat, and our lives are the voyage. If we are to sail intelligently we will need to get used to a different kind of map. It provides this kind of information:

- *Depth contours.* As a land map shows the contours of the land and its height above sea level, so a nautical chart shows the contours of the land below the water, and its depth below sea level. In terms of our spiritual journey, we could compare these two kinds of map to our outer and visible lives—the land map reveals the bits that we, and everyone else can see, with their achievements and their aims, while the ocean chart is a guide to our inner, and largely invisible, lives with their varying degrees of depth.

- *Submerged hazards such as wrecks and rocks.* Our inner journey likewise conceals such hazards. We can use our experience to help us notice where and what they are so that we can avoid being wrecked on them.

- *Ocean movements such as eddies, tidal rips, and hazardous currents.* These equate to the inner movements that we might notice as regular features of our inner journey. Over time we can learn to recognize what they are and where they are coming from, learning to work with or around them.

- *Visible navigation aids such as lighthouses, buoys, or prominent rocks and other landmarks along the coastline.* What external aids help guide our inner journey?

- *Recommended shipping routes.* Our inner chart might help us plot our preferred routes in prayer and discernment, noticing what has helped us in the past, while keeping an open mind about how these routes might evolve in the future.

So how might this translate into something that we can create and use in our spiritual voyaging? You might like to reflect on any or all of the following questions as you seek to become familiar with the chart of your inner landscape:

- As you review your lived experience, which parts of that experience seem, to you, to take you deep into the core of who you really are, and which, if any, feel shallow and affect you only on the surface of yourself? What moves you deeply, and what leaves you virtually untouched? What stirs up profound reactions? What makes you soar with joy or cry with pain, and what leaves you indifferent? For example, your relationship with a particular person may take you deep, while your daily work at the office may feel shallow in comparison. A particular issue may evoke a passionate response, while a committee meeting leaves you feeling apathetic. Or, of course, it may be the other way round. There will probably be considerable fluctuations in your reactions at different seasons of your life, and there will certainly be varying degrees of depth between different aspects of your life. This kind of reflection makes it possible to discern something of the hidden contours of your invisible inner life.

- From your experience of life so far, especially in its invisible dimensions, what has been the nature of the worst hazards you have encountered? For example, what things consistently tempt you to sail off course or to abandon your deepest dreams for the sake of lesser distractions? What memories haunt you like submerged wrecks, threatening the stability of your boat? What unresolved issues in your life keep lurking up out of the fog like rocks to lure you into shipwreck?

- What inner movements do you detect in your heart that tend to lead you closer to a sense of "living true" and what movements tend to pull you off course? For example, are there any particular lines of thought or ways of doing things that habitually encourage you to fix your gaze beyond yourself and your immediate concerns, and out toward the whole of God's creation? Are there any thought patterns or emotional slipstreams that tend to draw you in upon yourself, thus losing the wider perspective?

- Where, or who, are the landmarks that help you find your way? What gives you light in your darker times? Who has a habit of bobbing up just when you need someone, with the encouraging signal,

"It's OK. Keep going!"? Where are the rocks of steady assurance that help you trust your course?

- What shipping routes tend to bring you closer to God? For example, do you prefer a particular approach to prayer? Does it help you to share your journey with someone else, either an individual or a group of like-minded friends? Do particular books, or forms of liturgy help you? Do music, poetry, paint, or clay help you express your innermost longings and needs in prayer? These are your shipping routes. Rejoice in them, but remain always open to discover new channels.

Like land maps, or perhaps even more so, nautical charts become out of date very quickly and need to be frequently updated if they are to be useful. Our inner charts need updating in the light of the experience of every new day. Every period of prayer or meditation, every moment of our lived experience, will add new wisdom to the inner chart, warn us of fresh hazards, open us to new routes, reveal new depths. We can do this updating simply by taking time on a regular basis to be still and reflect on what is going on in our lives, where God is present to us and where God appears to be guiding us. For more help in this kind of reflective prayer, see also the companion volume *Taste and See.*

Reflect

Take time, if you feel drawn to do so, to construct a chart along these lines of your inner life as you currently perceive it, showing your depth contours, any hazards and helps, any inner movements you recognize, and any shipping lanes you find helpful. Use any medium that is helpful: words or images, paint or clay, or simply your own imagination.

You might like to begin with a broad brush chart that expresses an overview of how you see yourself "from the inside." This overview chart might show, for example, the main harbors you like to visit, and the places where you feel

you can drop anchor when you need to. You can then zoom
in, if you wish, on a more detailed aspect of your journey
as it is right now; for example, a particular issue you are
dealing with or a particular direction you are searching for.
These more detailed charts will show the same kind of data,
as applied to a specific matter that you are currently trying
to discern.

Where are we going?

Life on earth can often be hard and painful. Maybe because of
this, we cherish some kind of vision of a "heaven" where all will be
well, in some hoped-for life to come. And so, traditionally, if a Christian is asked where their life is headed, they would probably answer,
"Heaven."

If we see this "heaven" as our destination, our aim in life becomes
focused on making sure we eventually gain entry to it, even though
we would be hard-pressed to say just what we think we mean by
"heaven." Life on earth can then become merely a matter of surviving
and coping until something better appears beyond the horizon. And
there is no shortage of those who will sell us their passports. "Live
according to my rules," they will tell us, "and you will be 'saved.'"
How can we know whether these ways of thinking really have their
origins in God, or whether they are simply man-made ways of keeping people under control?

Yet the mystics, past and present, often remind us that heaven is
here and now, and not some reward given for a life well lived. And
Jesus declared that he had come "so that we might have life in all its
fullness." This doesn't sound like just a way of coping until we get to
where we are really going, but rather a way of actually bringing this
heaven into being, not just for ourselves but for all creation. Even as
we pray for "the coming of the Kingdom" we are either hastening or
delaying its fulfillment in every choice we make along the way, and
in every way we react to the circumstances of our daily living.

Nevertheless, it seems a strange thing to do, to set sail across an
uncharted sea without any real idea of our intended destination. One
thing that helps me to do just this is my recollection of another piece

of advice that Jesus gave us—to "become as little children." Little children embark upon life's journey with absolutely no sense of there being any destination. They just get on with it, living each day as it comes, dealing with each new encounter, negotiating each new relationship, rejoicing in each new discovery, learning from each new experience of pain. What they are actually doing is growing, and becoming. They are in process. They are evolving into who they truly are, the person God dreamed of when God created them.

Growing. Evolving. Becoming. These possibilities give a rather different "take" on the question of the destination. Heaven, seen in this light, might then be something more like "the wholeness of each of us within the wholeness of all creation." This changes the set of questions we need to ask from the traditional: "What must I do to be granted entry into heaven?" (with all the convoluted answers that that might lead us into) to "How can I most effectively engage in and cooperate with this process of becoming who I truly am, before and in God?"

For our boat, this translates into "How can I sail the seas of my life's circumstances in ways that help me grow into the wholeness I seek, for myself and for all creation?" The growing and becoming will be happening as we sail. They are not some distant target that we have to work toward attaining. The destination will look after itself, if we attend lovingly and discerningly to the moment we are living, as we are living it, just as a little child would do.

Viewed from this angle, the destination doesn't lie for ever beyond the horizon, but it evolves:

- through everyone we meet as we journey

- through every incident and encounter of our daily lives

- through every word of praise and every word of criticism we receive

- through every failure as well as through every achievement

- through everything that moves us, shocks us, attracts us, challenges and changes us

- in short . . . through everything that happens to us as we sail.

The voyage itself is our personal part of the eternal story that is unfolding through the eons of time. We each have a unique role to play in the telling of this Eternal Story. We each make a difference to its unfolding.

Can we let God launch us upon such a journey? Can we let God keep on and on relaunching us upon every new day of that journey? We might go down to the lakeside and discover our own life's boat riding at anchor there, in a scene that is based on an incident described in Luke 5:1–11. You might like to place yourself in the situation of the fisherman as you reflect on it, and notice your own feelings at the train of events as if this boat were your boat. If you feel drawn to do so, engage in your own conversation with the teacher who has stepped so unexpectedly into your boat.

It was a busy, vibrant scene at the lakeside. The new teacher was there again. His reputation had gone ahead of him, and everyone from miles around was clamoring to get a glimpse of him and listen to every word he said. There was talk that he was a man who could change lives, and there were very few people around who didn't feel that their lives needed changing in one way or another. Most of the men and women gathered that morning on the shore would have said, if you could have asked them, that they were looking for something more in their lives than simply surviving and keeping the rules, keeping their noses clean and not sticking their heads above the parapet, especially not in this occupied territory, where it didn't do to stand out in the crowd.

Yet, there was more . . . and this young teacher seemed to know what they were thinking better than they knew it themselves. There was something in his words and his demeanor that suggested quite different possibilities of finding that elusive "more," that didn't make use of the blunt instrument of armed revolt against the occupying powers.

As usual, there were fishermen at the edge of the lake. They were cleaning their nets, and they, too, were listening to the teacher, but perhaps with half their minds on the abysmal fruits of last night's fishing trip.

Then something quite unplanned and unexpected happened. The teacher walked down the beach and climbed right into one of the fishing boats, cool as you please! It seemed like a minor matter to the crowds. But to the fisherman whose boat it was it was the very last thing he was expecting. Suddenly the whole morning took on a very different hue. And the teacher, not content with stepping into the boat, then calmly asked the fisherman to push out a little way into the lake.

You could almost hear his unspoken protest: "Whose boat is this actually? Do I decide where she goes, or do you, an uninvited guest?" But the fisherman bit back his words and let the teacher move in.

The few meters' distance from the shore gave the teacher a much better range from which to address the crowds. Even the disgruntled fisherman could see that. The few meters of water didn't separate the teacher from his audience, but served somehow to connect him to them more effectively. Now they could all see him, and hear him. But in the fisherman's mind the struggle went on: "Since when has my boat been your soapbox? I have a job to do here, and I can't hang about all day while you occupy my boat." But again, the words remained unspoken, and instead, he began to listen more deeply to what the teacher was actually saying. It made sense. More so than he cared to admit to himself. Maybe his little boat was serving a useful purpose after all.

Eventually the teacher finished speaking, and turned to the fisherman. He didn't waste words:

"Put out into the deeper water now," he urged him, "and let down the nets for a catch."

A torrent of arguments gathered in the fisherman's mind. "Do you think you know how to do my job better than I do? You don't seem to understand what a dismal night it's been. There are no fish. This is a pointless exercise. And anyway, it's my boat!"

It was almost as though the teacher could read his mind. Suddenly the fisherman felt unaccountably ashamed of his unspoken reactions. Perhaps there was something in all of this. In spite of himself, he turned the boat round, headed out to the deeper waters, and let down the nets. And yes! The catch nearly sank the boat. Panic-stricken, the fisherman hailed across the water to his friends to come and give him a hand. There was no way he could handle this turn of events on his own. In no time, their boats, too, were almost sinking under the weight of all the fish.

Whatever the fisherman had thought he was searching for, as he listened to the teacher's words back there on the shoreline, he had found it, and much, much more of it than he knew how to deal with. His life had taken off at speed in new directions. His heart had been plunged into unguessed-at depths. His immediate instinct was to back off:

"Leave me, Lord," he whispered. "I can't handle this. I'm such a mess. Leave me."

The words came quietly back on the morning breeze:

"Don't be afraid," the teacher murmured. "This is only the beginning. Your life will know quite new realms of fruitfulness and discovery from now on, and you will become a guide for others. Trust me. Carry me in your boat, and let me carry you."

Silently, thoughtfully, the fisherman and the teacher gazed at each other, and then turned their sights to the horizon. The teacher moved toward the bow of the boat and took hold of the oars. And the fisherman followed him.

CHAPTER

Navigating the High Seas

The launch is perhaps a distant memory now. It seems like a long time since you had sight of land. The seas around you, your life's circumstances, the ups and downs, or maybe the flat calms and the tidal waves, have brought you to somewhere that can feel like the middle of nowhere. How do you find your way on this voyage, surrounded, it would appear, by miles of emptiness and no visible waymarks? If your spiritual journey feels a bit like this, maybe it's time to look for a few navigation aids.

The wreck of the *Association*

Ironically, one of humankind's most important navigation aids owes its origins to a major sea disaster. We begin this leg of our journey by going back in imagination to a foggy night on 22 October 1707 just off the south west coast of England. The English fleet of twenty-one sailing ships is under way, under the command of Admiral Sir Clowdisley Shovell, following the flagship, the *Association*. The official navigators on board the *Association* think the fleet is heading safely for home port, but one of the flagship's crew has been doing his own calculations. He realizes that the fleet is in fact heading for disaster on the Scilly Islands, and alerts the admiral. For his trouble he is hanged for mutiny, because in the Royal Navy of this time it is a capital offence to engage in "subversive navigation." A few hours later the *Association* and three further ships of the fleet run aground on the rocks of the Scillies with an almost total loss of life.

This particular incident was one of many disasters at sea that occurred largely because sailors of the time had no way of calculating their longitude position. Latitude was easy. The lines of latitude ran round the globe, parallel to the equator, showing you how far north or south you were. If your route was such that this was all you needed to plot your course, you could be fairly sure of a safe passage by observing the given latitudes, or "parallels." These were easy enough to gauge using sun and stars as guides. However, these fixed parallels were in no way adequate as navigational aids to the increasing numbers of ships steering their courses, in trade and at war, all over the oceans of the world. Many such ships were being lost. The loss of the *Association* was the final straw, and as a result the problem of calculating longitude moved to center stage. Sailors urgently needed to be able to calculate how far east or west they were at any given point, and only longitude could provide this information. The problem was well understood. Only a practical solution was lacking. In 1714 the Longitude Act was passed in Britain, offering a prize of £20,000 to the person who could come up with a reliable and practical method of measuring longitude.

Spiritual "latitude" and "longitude"

How does this shed any light on our need to discern our position and direction on our spiritual journeying?

I first came across the fascinating story of the longitude question through the story of John Harrison, who solved the longitude problem, as recounted in the book *Longitude* by Dava Sobel and William J. H. Andrewes. As I read their account I began to notice definite similarities with my own struggles to find my way when I feel at sea on my inner journey.

Like the oceangoing ships of the seventeenth and eighteenth centuries, I felt I knew about the latitudes. Many of us have grown up knowing about them, or have been taught them when we first made a spiritual commitment to follow a life of faith. There are a number of latitudes that act as guidelines for our spiritual journey. Depending on your faith tradition, these guidelines may emphasize the study of sacred scripture, observance of Sunday liturgy, moral precepts upon which we all agree, and adherence to established and accepted doctrines and creeds. Most of the people who don't come from any faith tradition also live by moral guidelines of this nature. These lines of latitude are fine, and fairly easily accessible, and provided that we stay within a limited range of prescribed shipping lines, they will guide us soundly.

What the longitude story tells me, however, is that there is a second dimension to our navigational needs. If we could find our way with the additional benefit of using this second, longitudinal, dimension in our journeying, we would have the means to navigate our way in uncharted waters and to make journeys that are not constrained by the official guidelines. The use of this second dimension would give us a whole new freedom to experience God's creation and thereby come closer to its creator.

We might compare the lines of latitude to our official belief system, as observed in public worship and the formal practice of our faith, while the lines of longitude invite us into a more direct relationship with God, such as can be discovered in personal prayer and discernment of the best course to steer through our own life's circumstances, wherever and whatever they happen to be. The two go together. The first guides our heads, the second opens up our hearts. To denigrate one and extol the other is to stray into danger. The secret seems to lie in finding the balance between them, allowing each to complement the other in our onward voyaging.

For many people, the faith community and the scriptures provide the "latitude" readings, but to travel true we also need a personal alignment—the longitude. It isn't enough just to know "what happened then" or "what 'they' say I should believe." We also need to learn to discover where God is for us here and now, and what God means for us personally in this place. And when we have discovered it, we need to trust it and act on it. It's a challenge, to discern our true alignment, but the story of the search for longitude shows us that we need a fixed point that we can trust absolutely, against which we measure all our movement. For us this fixed point is God who is both within us and beyond us.

Finding your longitude position

To calculate your longitude position aboard ship you need to know two things:

1. the time aboard ship

2. the time at the home port (or some other place of known longitude)

With these two items of data, the ship's navigator checks his position each day by:

resetting the ship's clock to local noon

consulting the home port clock

calculating the difference

Every hour's difference indicates fifteen degrees longitude, which can then be plotted on the chart. The ship's exact location is then known.

How might this translate into the language of our spiritual journey? What strikes me most forcibly in the analogy is that the two items of data required are the time where we are, and the time at the home port. In other words, this process of discernment (which is the term we might use to describe our spiritual navigation) is about two important factors:

- Where we actually are, in the tossing, changing circumstances of our daily living, and

- Where we find our fixed point, our home port, our pole star, the ground of our being, the true center of gravity around which our life spins.

We could even name these two factors as our relationship with the God who dwells continually within us (the immanent God) and our relationship with the God who is eternally beyond us (the transcendent God).

But how do we begin to read this kind of data? What does it mean in practice? The methods of the old seafarers can give us some useful clues:

- We can begin by reading the time in our own boat. What is actually going on in our daily living? How does it all feel? Where do we think we are headed and what is important to us right now? What issues are concerning us? These are all material for prayer, bringing the here and now first to our own consciousness and then, deliberately, into the presence of God.

- We can reset the time in our boat each day to the local noon. We do this by coming to stillness, noticing the still point, when the sun is at its highest, in the local place, in the here and now, the cut and thrust of every day. In practice this might mean taking a little time each day (it doesn't have to be at noon!) just to check in with God and reflect with God on what is happening around and within us. It happens where we actually are, not where we wish we were, or where we think we ought to be. This is about tuning into God's presence in the earthed reality of our lived experience, just as it really is.

- Finally, we consult the time at the home port. We do this by returning, in prayer to the deepest desires of our heart, to the longings that keep us aligned to the God beyond us, to that axis of love that defines both our own center of gravity and the center of gravity of all creation. One way of expressing this is to ask ourselves "What does the deepest core of my being say about this? How does the best in me react?" We will look at one method of doing this in a few moments.

An example might help to illustrate the process.

Let's imagine that my boat is sailing through a mixture of storms and calm, not too sure whether it is on course. I have recognized that my destination is about becoming who I most truly am, but I'm very unsure about whether I am getting closer to that destination in my daily living, or drifting further and further away from the course my true self most deeply desires.

The day dawns, and I go off to work. There is a problem in the office. I get irritated, and frustrated when no one seems to see things my way. I snap at my colleagues, and by the afternoon I am in a pretty black mood. When I get home I put my feet up for a while, read the paper, and take a walk down the garden. The peacefulness of the evening calms my spirits. Then a friend phones, simply to ask how I'm feeling, and has the grace to listen for ten minutes while I tell her! By the time I get to bed I feel more like myself, and tomorrow, God willing, I will be ready for whatever is round the next corner.

Now let's apply a little navigation science to this kind of day.

The time on board my boat has swung all over the place. My moods have ranged through irritability and frustration to peace, gratitude, and collectedness. This has been the reality of my day. It won't help to deny it or try to sanitize it. That is how things have been. But I can reset my ship's clock to the local noon. I take a few minutes simply to acknowledge before God the varying reactions of the day. I notice, in the stillness, those matters that made me agitated, and those incidents that brought me back to myself. I simply notice them, without any kind of judgment. This is my way of saying to God, "This is the here and now of my day, Lord. This is the only place I can begin to discern where my boat is going."

Finally, I let the stillness draw me down to my deepest roots, where the center of gravity of my own living is aligned with the center of gravity of all life, whom we call God. If I can allow myself to enter these deeper layers of my being, it becomes clear to me which of the day's events and reactions were coming from the true me and which were actually nudging me away from the core of my being. I notice, perhaps, that the time in the garden in the evening calm and the time in conversation with my friend were indicators of my true direction. They were helping me to grow more truly into who I am. The antagonisms in the office, however, had their roots in a less authentic part of me—the part that wants to win arguments and gain kudos by getting people to do what I want. The time at the home port is the place where I discern these truths. And it is the means by which I can measure my day's course and discover the extent to which I have been living true today, and the ways in which I have departed from my own deepest truth. With this information, I can make adjustments to my course if necessary—for example, by taking more time to be peaceful in the garden, more time to be with my friends, and by trying consciously to direct less of my energy to scoring points in the office.

A steady clock amid the confusion

The reason that we celebrate John Harrison's unlikely contribution to the search for a method of calculating longitude is not because of his understanding of the heavens, but because of his clock!

Harrison was an unknown and unschooled country craftsman from the North of England with a passion for clocks. The scientific minds of the times had fixed themselves on the notion that the secret of longitude must lie in the heavens. If only mankind could learn to map the heavens, the mystery of navigating the seas would be solved. Harrison brought some lateral thinking to bear on the problem, and insisted that what was needed was a clock that would give a precise time reading at sea, no matter how long or stormy the voyage. This clock would provide the key to maintaining that subtle alignment between the time at sea and time at the home port. It was a masterpiece of balance and precision, a unique achievement of its age. Now, of course, the same effect can be achieved with a wristwatch, but Harrison's clock was to open the first gateway to safer shipping, and it might also lead us into a deeper understanding of how to find our way through life in line with what our hearts know to be God's way too.

The clock's character can perhaps be summed up as "equilibrium amid turbulence." Its design made it possible to maintain an accurate time reading even when the ship was pitching and tossing in Atlantic storms or in the throes of naval battle and cannon fire. The whole story tells me that to find my way across the oceans of life, I will be helped more by the gift of finding a still point within myself than by scanning "the heavens" for signposts—a skill in any case not easily practiced in regions where there is often cloud and fog, a description that certainly fits the state of my heart very frequently. There is a strong parable here for the inner journey and how we find our way on it. The answer doesn't lie in the heavens, nor is it confined to knowledge in the minds of the experts. It is for each of us to discover and use for ourselves.

So the secret comes back to stillness. In the stillness of reflective prayer we will make our first and most crucial steps toward ongoing spiritual discernment. For more guidance on ways of developing the habit of reflective prayer you might like to look at the companion volume *Taste and See*, or at one of the books listed in the bibliography. For help in cultivating the art of inner balance, see also *Landmarks*.

A visit to the bat barn

How do we establish this subtle alignment between our own truest self and the True Life of God? It all sounds like a pipe dream. But I would suggest that in fact we don't need to establish it at all. It is always there. We merely need to learn to tune in to it and become aware of it.

A story I once heard helps me to see how this might happen. The story described a barn full of bats. The parent bats had nested there, and the baby bats were just beginning their lives, hanging on the rafters. Hundreds and hundreds of baby bats were in residence. The parents went off to search for food, and eventually returned to the barn to feed their offspring. Now, how, in that chaos of baby bats, all hanging there in the dark and squeaking for their supper, did the parents ever find their own young?

The answer is remarkable. Each bat, it seems, has its own unique note that communicates between the baby and the parent to signal, "Here I am!" The parent returning with the food only has to tune in to the familiar note of its own offspring, and the connection is made instantly.

With this story fresh in my mind, I came across a few lines from a poem by Gerard Manley Hopkins shortly afterward. It read as follows:

> Let me be to Thee as a circling bird,
> Or bat with tender and air-crisping wings
> That shapes in half-light his departing rings,
> From both of whom a changeless note is heard.

Hopkins goes on to say that for him "the authentic cadence was discovered late" but that now "I have found the dominant of my range."

We too may find that it has taken us most of a lifetime to sense the presence of that "changeless note," but that once recognized, it is seen to be the unique note that links the God within us directly to the God beyond us.

St. Paul says something similar:

> The Spirit comes to help us in our weakness. For when we cannot choose words in order to pray properly, the Spirit himself expresses our plea in a way that could never be put into words, and God who knows everything in our hearts knows perfectly well what he means. (Romans 8:26–27, Jerusalem Bible)

The fixed point is within us, as well as beyond us, as Paul reminds us. The indwelling Holy Spirit enables us to discern our true alignment, where the God within us is tuned to the God beyond us. This is our inner compass always there to help us to discern our own true north. The God within us dwells in our hearts, giving us a sense of harmony when we are living true to ourselves, and warning us with a sense of unease when we are being untrue to ourselves. The God beyond is present to us like a lighthouse, beaming out a unique signal that is meant just for us, revealing Godself in the events and in the people around us, and in the whole of creation.

We tune in to this changeless note that is uniquely connecting each of us with God by learning to live reflectively. In the earlier example we considered, the moments of centeredness, such as the time in the garden and with the friend, were times when the changeless note was audible. The times of fretfulness and irritability were more like spiritual interference on our personal waveband with God. But the only way to learn how to tune into this waveband is to actually do it. We can also begin to develop the habit of checking out our dealings with other people against "the changeless note." In what aspects of our relating to others do we feel that we are being true to ourselves, and are there any aspects of the relationships, or of our immediate reactions to people, that leave us feeling uneasy?

Reflect

Take a few moments every so often, in whatever you are doing, and try to notice whether you can discern the changeless note.

Notice whether your heart is at rest and in a state of balance, whatever turbulence there may be all around you. Like Harrison's clock, your heart is designed for such fine tuning. God will hear and respond to the innermost cries of your heart just as the parent bat hears the squeak of its own young. The waveband is always open. Only the interference of our own inner turbulence and distractedness blocks the reception.

The pole star within us

In her book *The Celtic Spirit,* Caitlín Matthews invites her readers to reflect on the view we have of the circling heavens on a clear night, with the fixed point of the pole star (the North Star) around which all others stars appear to be in motion. This is how she describes it:

> If we could set up a stop-frame of the solar year and point it up toward the northern heavens, we would see revealed the dance of the circumpolar stars about the pole star in a fantastic circle dance. Among the peoples of the north, the pole star is called "the nail of heaven" because of its unchanging position in the sky: an unfailing and welcome guide to travelers and sailors in the darkest night. Discovering our own true north as the compass point of our soul's direction is a worthwhile enterprise on our spiritual path.

We could think of "the nail of heaven" as an invisible axis around which all creation revolves in balance and harmony. This axis around which creation spins is also the axis around which our own hearts revolve, when we are living true. Perhaps another way of looking at the challenge of hearing the changeless note is to seek to find our own true alignment with this invisible axis. I suggest that we know when we are living true to this alignment—we have all experienced times or events in our lives when we simply knew that we were in the right place at the right time, doing whatever it was that we knew we had to do, or holding back from doing what we intuitively knew it would be unwise to do. And even though few of us will be in this true alignment for most of our time, once we know how it feels, it becomes more likely that we will be able to tune into it, as to a compass at the very heart of our being. This compass picks up every vibration, and works through our bodies, minds, and spirits. We can learn to listen to the tensions and flutters that our bodies register. We can learn to notice what makes our minds buzz like gadflies and what draws them into calm and balance. We can learn to recognize what stirs our spirits and energizes our soul's journey, and what stifles and subdues us. With such a compass we can gradually learn how to sail true to ourselves, and the essential practice comes through the habit of reflective living.

I was reminded of the importance of this inner alignment with the axis of life when I was helping with a training weekend for people who were preparing to accompany others in their prayer during retreats. Several of them, understandably, commented on how inadequate they felt, listening as another person shared something of their prayer journey, and on a sense of helplessness to offer any kind of guidance. We all knew, of course, that prayer companionship is not about guidance, and that the only guide in the process is the Holy Spirit. I reminded them of this, and urged them to remember that the Holy Spirit is actually and powerfully present in every encounter.

After they had dispersed, I was thinking over what I had said. I knew it was true, but I also knew how inadequate a comment it had been. As if the Holy Spirit were like a driving instructor, I thought to myself, sitting in the passenger seat and ready to jam on the brakes if the human companion gets things wrong. Had I been unwittingly domesticating the creator of trillions of galaxies, I wondered? The more I thought about it, the more depressed I became, and it took me only a couple of hours before I sought out my own mentor, and told him how pathetically inadequate I was feeling myself, and that I felt the time had come to stop doing this kind of work, let alone training other people to do it. It was at this nadir of confidence that my mentor made a comment I shall never forget:

"What's really important isn't what you say or what you teach," he told me. "What really matters is that you yourself are trying to live true to the deepest alignment of your soul to God. When the prayer companion is living true, then nothing needs to be said. That true axis becomes an attractor to encourage the other person to seek out their own deepest alignment, though the companion will probably be completely unconscious of it. This is what makes the relationship fruitful and life-giving. This is what gives God space to be God."

Beacons, true and false

Most of us know people like this, who, we feel, are, deep down, living true to themselves (though they may often get things wrong too). Such people liberate our own souls to do likewise, and give us the encouragement we need to trust the deepest alignment and make our life choices with reference to that innermost compass. Such people can be lighthouses for us as we navigate life's seas. They beam out a steady signal—their own personal changeless note—and these signals can help us to steer our boat. Like the bats, every lighthouse has its own code of light signals, so that seafarers can ascertain where they are relative to known hazards such as rocks or sandbanks.

Often our "lighthouse people" are found in exposed and rocky places themselves. They may be people who have struggled with difficult circumstances and found a way of living true to their own changeless note in the process. You wouldn't expect to find a lighthouse in the middle of a sheltered grassy meadow. So look for your lighthouses where there is, or has been, turbulence and trouble, and take time to touch into that steady alignment that helps them to stand firm in that place and to beam out trustworthy signals to others.

Reflect

Do you have any lighthouses in your life? Who are they, and what is it about them that enables you to trust their steady signals?

Our own experience can also be a true beacon to us, reminding us of times in the past when we knew we were living true, and helping us to steer by that truth again in a changed situation. At one of the Greenbelt Festivals, the theme was "The Kiss of Life," and an underlying question was "In what ways does God give us the 'kiss of life'?" Participants were encouraged to remember the ways they felt they had personally felt such a "kiss of life" restoring them to right relationship with themselves and with God. For me the memory that stood out most vividly was simply the experience of being listened to, with loving, nonjudgmental, whole-hearted attention, when I needed to pour out my heart to God. That experience, during a time of crisis, made God real for me in ways that no amount of doctrine ever could. It is an experience I can always go back to, seeking such a loving listener if I need to, and trying to be such a loving listener, if another pilgrim needs a listening place.

Reflect

What experiences in your own life still shine out in the darkness like beacons that can continue to guide your path?

But not all beacons mean well toward us. Some can be seducing us onto dangerous rocks. I was shocked to learn, when reading about the story of how the early lighthouses were constructed around our shores (in *The Lighthouse Stevensons* by Bella Bathurst), that one of the most intractable problems was not so much the very high cost as the action of the so-called "wreckers." These were people who lived along the remote shorelines and made their living from what came ashore from wrecked boats. They had a vested interest in keeping up the level of shipwrecks, and were hostile to any plans to make shipping safer. In the worst cases, they might even light false beacons on dangerous promontories to seduce seafarers into a false sense of safety, while actually luring them to their deaths. Perhaps only experience and the benefit of hindsight can help us discern any "false beacons" in our own lives. Once discerned, however, they can and must be avoided, and if appropriate, other travelers should be warned of them.

Life today lights many a false beacon along our ways, some more lethal than others. Examples include advertising that seduces us, or our children, into consuming substances that may harm us, or engaging in activities which are well known to be addictive, or the beacon that lures us onto the rocks of burnout, breakdown, and family dysfunction by beaming out the false promise that the more money we earn the happier we will be.

Reflect

Have you fallen foul of any false beacons like this, or can you see their dangerous lights anywhere around you? If so, how would you want to avoid them in the future, and perhaps warn others of the dangers?

The still center

A familiar story from the life of Jesus can take us to the heart of the matter of finding a steady and true alignment amid all the stress. The story appears in all the synoptic gospels (Matthew 8:23–27, Mark 4:35–41, and Luke 8:22–25). Try reading one of these accounts of a sudden squall over the Sea of Galilee. Imagine yourself on board that little boat. As you read it, try to enter into the reality of it, and let it become a squall in your own life. It may be something you are grappling with even as you read. Or it may be the memory of a stormy passage you have had at some point, or even a storm you are fearing in the future. Take your memories, your anxieties or your fears on board the boat with you, and let them whip up the seas of your life in whatever ways come to mind.

Your ship is tossing mercilessly now, and the winds are ripping through your sails. You may feel that you have lost control of the journey altogether. But at the back of the boat someone is sleeping like a baby, untouched by the turmoil all around him. Just notice that stillness, that peace, that trust. He is the one who can change things, but are you going to wake him up?

What does this sleeping figure mean for you? He reminds me of poor old John Harrison, trying to carry out the sea trials of his steady clock amid raging storms, seasickness, cannon fire, and the bluster of the crew all around him. But the clock's pendulum runs true. It is the only way to get on course and stay on course. Are you going to consult it? Listen to Jesus' words, when his frantic friends finally wake him up. Addressing the wild elements, both in the winds and water and in the hearts of his friends, he says: "Be still." And then, as the storm subsides, the gentle challenge: "Why are you so afraid? Why won't you trust my presence in the depths of your heart, steadily connecting you to everything you need?"

Steering a true course "in real time"

You have probably come across your own version of the story of the man who was walking down the street one day. He saw a sign warning passersby to beware of falling masonry, and so he made sure he kept an eye on the activity going on at the top of the surrounding high-rise buildings. And after a few minutes, he fell down a manhole.

In our soul's navigation, too, we can lose the balance between our need to be in alignment with the transcendent God and our need to be in touch with the state of the seas all around us. We can keep our eyes fixed on the heavens to such an extent that we miss what is underneath our own noses.

In its own way, the story of John Harrison's determined search for a means of measuring longitude is an apt illustration of this danger. While the fellows of the Royal Society and the best scientific minds of the age were totally convinced that the answer lay "in the heavens," and that if they could map the skies, they would learn to find their way on earth, John Harrison was looking at the problem from a very different, and much more down-to-earth angle. He came up against heavy resistance, as his story reveals. He was seen as something of a threat to the learned minds who thought their way must be the only way to crack the longitude problem. This man from the country, this simple craftsman, was certainly not top of the ratings with the leaders of scientific and political opinion of his times. There may be parallels here with the experience of the spiritual seafarer who is searching for personal bearings in the oceans of life. The custodians of the lines of latitude may feel threatened by those who question the assumption that all the answers are stored safely in the bishop's filing cabinet. They may regard our personal discernment as subversive navigation or even mutiny. Let us not be deterred by that kind of resistance, any more than John Harrison was blown off course in his own search. Let us remember that subversive navigation could have saved the *Association*, if the admiral had listened to the mutinous sailor instead of hanging him.

What Harrison seems to have seen, that eluded most others of his time, was the difficulty of getting a steady reading on board a tossing boat. While the Royal Society was stargazing, he was attending to the immediate problems posed by the winds, tides, and currents, not to mention the occasional naval battle. How can his story help us further? How do we steer a true course "in real time," when the winds and tides are quite possibly against us, and when unseen currents may tug us where we never intended to go? How do we maintain that steady alignment with our own deepest truth, when everything around us is in a state of constant change and motion?

The tides of our inner movements

When I think of tides, I notice the sweeping inner movements in my life. Some of these tides carry me powerfully forward. Others have the potential to swamp me. I think of the flow tide energy I experience when, for example, I am engaged in work that feels worthwhile, or when a relationship is growing and developing fruitfully. And I think of the ebb tide experience, when, perhaps, I am locked into a destructive relationship or I am habitually being asked to do work that I don't feel has any value.

Tides are a bit like a moving walkway. If you move in the direction of the flow, your movement will be made easier and you will arrive faster. If you walk against the direction of flow, you will have a hard time and it will take you much longer to get to where you want to be. And if you try to go across the tidal walkway, you won't simply arrive on the opposite side, but you will have been carried some way upstream or downstream, depending on the speed and direction of the tide.

My inner movements, I find, can have the same kind of effect. So, instead of reacting to the feelings they engender as something I have to rise above, it might be more fruitful to try to tune into their energy. An experience of authentic powerful elation, for example, delivers a charge of positive energy. It is well worth hitching a ride on such a power pack, provided it is coming from the real core of ourselves and is running true to that core alignment we have already explored.

A movement that unsettles us, on the other hand, perhaps leaving us dejected or apathetic or in turmoil, can draw us off course, draining us of essential vital energy. Its effect can be to leave us feeling as though we are wading through treacle, or trying to walk up the down escalator. In this state of mind we are going to have to work against the effect of the tide.

Our moods and feelings, however fickle they may seem, can nevertheless be helpful pointers to these inner movements, but we need to sift them and reflect on what is really going on underneath the surface waves. For example, I have a serious aversion to unsolicited phone calls offering me double glazing, home improvements, car insurance, or whatever. I especially hate them when they disturb my peace just after six in the evening, when the calls may be cheaper but my dinner is on the plate! When a call like this comes through, I discover, rather to my shame, that I can be quite rude to the caller. One evening, after I had summarily dismissed a young woman who sounded like an answering machine message, asking me to have my house "improved," I did take a little time to reflect on why, exactly, I get so uptight about this kind of thing. She had interrupted my evening meal and made me listen to her patter, and I realized she had actually managed to put me in a bad mood.

Why would such a trivial occurrence have this kind of power? When I stopped to think about it, I began to notice that in fact I have a more general "inner movement" that is about a dislike of being interrupted. It has to do with people invading my space without my permission, and it shows itself in other ways, apart from the telephone phobia. This is what I mean by an underlying movement—in this case a negative one. My changing moods can point to it. I have a choice about what to do with it. Since this is a negative movement, the best in me wants to work against it and become more aware of what is really happening when I cut someone short on the phone, and even, perhaps, to address the real issues that are making me react like this.

But how can we know whether a powerful movement, either negative or positive, is coming from the core of our being or not? How can we tell whether to flow with it or work against it? Although much of the answer has, perhaps, to be trial and error, there is nevertheless some good news here. Many of those who have made this kind of soul voyage before us report the following observations:

- If, in the core of our being, we are seeking to live in alignment with all that is truest within us, then what we experience as a powerful flow tide can, in general, be trusted to be bringing us closer to the destination of who God has dreamed us to be, and the tides that generate feelings of unease will usually be indicating that we are running off course.

- If, on the other hand, we have made a fundamental choice not to live true to our deeper alignment, but, instead, perhaps, to pursue a life focused mainly on personal gain at the expense of the rest of creation, then this pattern appears to be reversed: the experience of elation may be signs that we are running further away from God's dream for us, while the feelings of discontent and unsettledness may be God's nudges to rethink our course.

We who are making this particular sea voyage are, by definition, spiritual voyagers, seeking to live true to the deepest core of our being, even though everyday events may frequently pitch us off course. It follows, therefore, that we can, in general, trust the strong and positive tides that move us on, and we can learn to work against the negative movements that tend to pull us off course.

Reflect

Reflect on some of the tidal movements in your own story. Remember especially any strong tidal drag or reaction that threatened to swamp you. How did you react? Now remember any tidal flow experience that has proved to be a blessing, sweeping you forward and helping you to grow spiritually. How did you react to that, and what effects has it had? In the light of these memories, how do you read the tidal movements that are around for you right now, and how will you choose to react—will you flow with, or work against them?

Running fast in order to stand still?

How often have I complained about this phenomenon! Or perhaps I have expressed it as "taking one step forward and two steps back." So I was surprised to discover, on board a boat I had the pleasure of inhabiting for a few days, that there was an indicator of both the actual speed of the vessel through the water and the "speed over ground" (the effective speed in terms of the distance, in nautical miles, or knots, being covered per hour). I was fascinated to learn that it is indeed actually possible to be moving forward at a rate of, say five knots, but because you are sailing against a tide which itself is moving at a rate of, say two knots, your actual speed over distance is only three knots, because of the drag of the tide. In theory, if you are sailing against a very fast-flowing tide, it would be possible to be moving backward! By contrast, if you are sailing with the tide, instead of against it, a boat speed of five knots could increase to an actual speed over distance of much more than this, because the tide would be adding to your speed and not dragging you back.

Perhaps the same is true when we are dealing with our deep inner movements. Those that have a negative effect and need to be worked against will inevitably appear to slow us down. Those that deliver a positive charge will appear to speed us up. So if I find myself struggling and getting nowhere fast, this may be an indication that I am indeed at present working "against the tide," that is, against a negative inner movement, and I need to accept the inevitable decrease in speed, or lack of any significant "progress." I must adjust my expectations to the situations I actually find myself in. Such labored times will be balanced by other periods in my life when the inner movements will carry me forward at speeds beyond anything I could achieve under my own steam.

The invisible currents

Along with the hazards of tidal movements, we also come up against the effects of deep, invisible underwater currents that can rip our vessel out of true, or can become an unexpected blessing on our voyage. Like the tides, these can have the effect of pulling us rapidly in a positive or a negative direction, like some unfathomable game of snakes and ladders.

Currents tend to be at their strongest where there is some kind of constriction, for example where water flows between rocks. In our spiritual journeying, we may be able to detect their presence with the benefit of hindsight, and it is a good idea to take time to notice any deep currents that our experience may have revealed. These might take the form of particular issues that habitually drag us off course. If anyone has ever warned you that you are "riding a hobby-horse," this might indicate the effects of stirrings within you that lie deeper than your conscious mind, and trigger strong reaction, or even overreaction.

On the other hand there can be life-giving currents, like the Gulf Stream, that bring us warmth and growth and vitality. Creative activity goes on like a deep undercurrent in our psyche all the time, and often makes its power felt in a wave of new inspiration when we are off guard. Perhaps you can recognize the presence of such streams in your life, maybe in the shape of special friends, or some form of work or play that revitalizes you, or memories of when fresh inspiration broke through your normal conscious thought processes.

And it has to be acknowledged that many of the currents that powerfully affect us all are invisible and inscrutable. There are currents of opinion that carry us along, sometimes against our better judgment. There are deep social and psychological currents that operate upon us subliminally, and can expose us to the manipulative influences of other people's controlling agendas. Examples of such currents include the subtle power of advertising, seducing us into a deeply ingrained consumer mentality and generating artificial "desires" that can seriously undermine our core desire to live God's dream, or the power of political indoctrination that (even in a so-called free democracy) can convince us that it might be right and necessary to diminish or destroy an individual or a minority group for the sake of national security. The power of such propaganda should not be underestimated.

A friend of mine was surfing in Australia when she was swept off her board and dragged under water by the undertow. She came close to drowning, and in these extreme moments, she recalls how she cast herself upon God in a prayer of surrender, fully expecting to die. In fact, her surrender meant that she stopped fighting her circumstances and acknowledged that the power of the undertow was beyond her control. This in turn released something in the situation and freed her from the downward drag. Sometimes we can feel caught in the undertow of prevailing destructive currents in our world, even though we cannot actually name them and feel powerless to counteract them. Sometimes we may have to stop struggling in our own strength and take our helplessness to God in a prayer of trustfulness, simply acknowledging our deep desire to live true and our awareness of all these currents that seem to be working against us.

So make use of both the tidal effects of your inner movements and the deeper currents that affect the ways you make your choices and decisions. Let their good energies carry you forward, but work against their effects to the best of your ability when they are pulling you off course or dragging you down. But do as sailors are advised to do: if you know that you are in a turbulent tidal zone right now, where your moods are fluctuating for whatever reason, or that you are at the mercy of dangerous currents, take an anchor, and use it, so that you can hold yourself steady from time to time to take stock of what is going on. This anchor is primarily time for prayer and reflection, time to be still with God at the ground of your being. But an anchorage may also be a friend with whom you can share your experience, or a place where you can reconnect to your own roots. We will look at the need for an anchor point in more depth in chapter 7.

The winds of circumstance

While the tides in my life tend to originate within me, and represent the inner movements and unconscious energies I experience, with all their potential to draw me on or drive me off course, the winds feel more like the outer circumstances, the effects of the simple nitty-gritty of daily life.

A wise sailor becomes familiar with the winds that are likely to make a difference to the course, especially the prevailing winds. Prevailing winds have a degree of predictability about them. Just as it is possible to identify the prevailing winds in a particular part of the earth, so we can perhaps also identify prevailing winds in our own personal circumstances.

Reflect

It might be helpful to be still for a moment and take a long cool look at what is around for you right now: the ongoing relationships, the tasks you are habitually occupied with, the kinds of questions and difficulties, but also the delights and encouragements that you have come to regard as part of what makes your life what it is. And then ask yourself these questions:

- *What tends to dominate your circumstances on a regular basis? This might be, for example, dealing with a difficult relationship, struggling in an unsatisfactory job, or, more positively, being deeply involved with a project that inspires you. Whatever you find will be matters that are engaging a large proportion of your energy. They are the prevailing winds of your spiritual voyage.*

- *Now look at whether these prevailing winds are helping you move on creatively, or are pulling you off course, or holding you back in your desire to become more truly who you are.*

If you are discovering any prevailing winds in your life that are draining you of energy and hampering your voyage, can you do anything to lessen their negative effects?

If you find prevailing winds that are blowing in your favor,
moving you on to where you desire to be, enjoy them, thank
God for them, and take full advantage of them.

The habit of reflective prayer, preferably on a daily basis, will help you to notice these prevailing winds, and to monitor the way you respond to them.

Gusts and wind changes

Wind speed and wind direction can change without notice. Something may happen out of the blue, or a word may be spoken, or a gesture observed that can pitch us into a completely new direction. The morning may have begun calmly, as we went about our normal tasks, then a letter arrives, or a phone call is received, and all at once we find ourselves consumed with anger, for example, or high with anticipation.

The same logic can be helpful here as in dealing with the more predictable winds in our lives. The fundamental question might be: Is this sudden wind change furthering my journey with God or is it hampering it? If the former, how can I run with it? If the latter, how can I work against it?

The only difference would be that these sudden shifts happen moment by moment. If we are to monitor them effectively, and use them or counteract them according to where they seem to be coming from, we need to be continually reflective. I once heard it said that true photographers don't just take photographs when they notice something worth photographing. They keep the shutter of their inner eye open all the time, constantly sifting the images that strike their retina, catching the extraordinary amid the ordinary. To live reflectively is to live like this—not obsessively analyzing everything that happens to us, but living with a high degree of awareness of the people, events, and movements all around us, catching the positive winds and standing firm against the gusts that might blow us over.

Using the rudder

Experienced sailors know better than to sail directly into the wind, or to aim straight for a visible destination, as though the ocean were some kind of motorway. At sea we have to listen to the immediate conditions as well as keeping our ultimate destination in mind. We need to maintain the proper balance between the boat, the sailor, and the sea. We might translate this into the need to discover and maintain the proper balance between ourself, our circumstances, and God.

The wind shifts continually, both in speed and direction, and we respond to this constant flux by using the rudder—not using brute force to impose our will upon the waves, but touching the tiller gently, so that we can feel the subtle shifts of wind force and currents, letting the boat itself show us what to do. The art is to be at home with the wind and the waves, to trust the movements of our circumstances, to trust the process through which we are becoming the person God is dreaming into being. To sail sensitively is to cooperate with that becoming, moment by moment, and to trust it.

Usually this means that we will get to where we want to be by indirect steps. It is often said that "God writes straight with crooked lines." The "crooked lines" are evident enough when we look back over any day's journeying. In sailing terms, they trace our tacking movements, backward and forward, right and left, negotiating each new twist and turn of our unfolding life situations, zigzagging our track through winds and currents. If we could take our bearings at any given point, we would usually discover that we are very far from traveling true north, and yet that deep underlying orientation remains the pole star that guides us, and, as Richard Bode says in his classic little book *First You Have to Row a Little Boat*:

> The truth is that there are destinations beyond destinations, and so the confirmed sailor goes on tacking forever.

So what is this rudder that gives us the power to steer a good course? The freedom of the seas is meaningless unless we learn to discern which direction is calling us. A boat without a rudder spells anarchy. Perhaps the rudder is our deepest, most authentic wisdom, which is also the indwelling presence of the Holy Spirit. It is what gives purpose and meaning to our lives. It is the way we implement the course changes that we find we need whenever we take our bearings in the silent stillness of prayer.

Reflect

What does the word "rudder" mean for you in your voyaging? What helps you to adjust your course when you sense that you are drifting out of true? One way to learn to use the rudder is to saturate yourself in the attitudes of Jesus, as revealed in the Gospels. In Jesus, Christians believe we can know and relate to a man who lived the True Life completely authentically, and continues to live it in us, through the Holy Spirit. A sustained exercise in getting in touch with the True Life in this way is offered in the companion volume Wayfaring.

While we will be adjusting our course continually, a radical change of course will be much less common. Perhaps we changed our course in this fundamental way when we became Christian, or first awoke to an awareness of the importance of God in our lives. For subsequent course-changing, one important guideline applies: never change a course that you set while you were focused on God and on your desire to become the person God is dreaming you to be, when you come to times when this focus slips. As a navigator, hold the true course that you knew was right when you could see the way ahead, even though the winds and currents pull you sideways or the clouds are down and the wind is against you.

At the end of the day, we can't force our circumstances into compliance with our will, any more than we can make the winds and waves obey us. What we can do, however, is learn to be in respectful relationship with them, adjusting our course to take the most creative, the most loving, the most Christ-like way forward at every shift of the tides, winds, and currents.

Let's end this part of the journey with a visit to a couple of sisters who are entertaining a welcome guest. Each of the sisters lives in our own heart, in some form, and so does the guest. Although this incident happens on dry land, between them, these three may shed quite a lot of light on our seafaring. The story is narrated in Luke 10:38–42. Try reading it through, slowly and reflectively, and entering into it in your imagination, as if it were your boat's cabin where the traveler is seeking rest.

The traveler had been on the road for quite a while. There had been a great many demands made upon him, and what he really needed right now was a bolt-hole, where he could spend some quality time with close friends who would give him space just to be himself for a little while. He made his way to Bethany, and knocked on the door of his good friends, Martha and Mary.

Martha came to the door. She was the one who invited him in and welcomed him. One might even say, she let him step "into her boat." He sat down and began to relax at once. But he could see that Martha was tense. He could read her mind, and what he read there made him sad: she was rapidly working out, in her head, what to do for supper, and whether there were enough tomatoes and peppers for a salad, and which kind of wine he might prefer. Everything that was buzzing round in her head was about how to make him comfortable. Couldn't she understand, he wondered, that what would really make him feel at ease would be for her to attend to simply being with him, rather than all the things she might do for him? But he didn't say anything. He understood her motives, and loved her for her attentive concern.

Eventually Martha disappeared into the kitchen, and the traveler sat quietly by the fire, thinking his own thoughts, and listening to the bustling sounds coming from the next room. It was then that the other sister came into the room, and greeted him warmly, sitting down at his feet, as though that were all she had ever wanted to do. He spoke to her. He told her about his travels, and about everything he had learned from the people he had met, and the way God was touching their lives. He shared with her his own deepest thoughts and feelings, and he listened to the echoes coming back to him from this gentle companion. Mary didn't say much. But she soaked up everything the traveler told her, and, mysteriously, began to see her own many problems in a rather different light.

The peaceful atmosphere was suddenly shattered. Martha was boiling over.

"I'm here in the kitchen doing all the work," she complained. *"At this rate there's not going to be any supper. Can't you tell Mary to come and give me a hand?"*

Ever so gently, the traveler took Martha's hand and drew her closer to him. Reluctantly, she sat down at his feet alongside her sister.

"Martha," he said, *"You are so anxious about all these things, and I appreciate all your work so much, but I really only came here to see you both. Let's just be together for a while. Everything else will fall into place then, you'll see."*

The Martha within us will always be harassed by the winds and tides and the high seas all around us. The Mary within us knows where the authentic center of our living is to be found, and goes there. The traveler makes us welcome, just as we are, when things are falling apart, and when things are falling into place. But we will hear him most clearly when we sit still and listen.

CHAPTER

5

Perils of the Deep

This chapter won't be plain sailing. Fraught as it is with choices and dilemmas, the voyage upon which we have embarked is not necessarily going to lead through the calm reaches of God's peace. This has never been the way of things for those who have sailed before us, including Jesus himself. Yet there are patterns we may learn to recognize and events we might to some extent anticipate if we consider a few strategies for dealing with some of the perils that may await us in the deeper waters of our spirit's journeying.

So we might usefully look at that aspect of our voyaging that exposes us to the various kinds of threat that the oceans may hold for fragile craft such as our lives represent.

Storm force

The most obvious hazard of the seas is the sudden and often violent power of storm, so we begin by looking at some of the things that tend to foment storm–force winds in our lives, and how we might deal with these storms when they arise. Storms at sea usually take us by surprise and challenge our seafaring skills to the limits. We can never really be prepared for them, but we can look back over our story and begin to notice the danger zones out of which turbulent seas seem to have arisen in the past. While this can never be a reliable prediction of what may happen in the future, it does give us a few clues about where storms might be expected in the times ahead.

Reflect

As you reflect on the possibilities mentioned, see whether any of them presses a button in your own memory bank. Have any of these factors precipitated inner storms for you in the past? Just notice what you find, and record it, as it were, in your inner "ship's log." Don't reproach yourself or others, or try to solve things. Begin simply by getting in touch with the kind of weather patterns and conditions that tend to throw you off course or capsize you.

- A sudden change of wind, catching you off guard. This may take any number of forms: an unexpected turn of events that demands a radical rearranging of your normal routine, triggered, perhaps, by bereavement, redundancy, or some other unwelcome change; the breakdown of a relationship or the loss of something or someone you depended upon; betrayal or abuse of some form by someone you trusted; or simple bad luck, with all its power to abort your dreams and expectations and undermine your assumptions and securities.

- The kind of heightened tension that results from what we might call "competition stress." Sailors in competitive events, for example, often run close to the limits of their own and their boats' endurance in the desire to win the race. Is it possible that some of the storms that blow up in our inner lives are self-inflicted in this way? Is an inordinate desire for achievement and recognition tempting us to push ourselves into a lifestyle that is fuelled almost entirely by adrenalin?

- Interpersonal conflict, or indeed, conflict on a larger scale, forcing us into different patterns of living. Private battles can drive us into an emotional desert, or turn home or office into a war zone. Global conflicts can turn us, overnight, into dispossessed refugees. The stately galleons of bygone centuries, no less than the battleships of the modern age, not only had to face the natural challenge of fickle ocean weather systems, but they had to do so under cannon fire or submarine or airborne attack.

How many of our inner storms have their origins in a knot of conflict that we are unable to resolve and which pitches us into high seas whenever we get entangled in it? If this is true for you, can you locate and name the source of that conflict?

- Stormy times of life, such as adolescence, the mid-life years, or the declining years when anxiety can be hugely magnified. Mariners know the terrors of the Roaring Forties, the waters that lie between the latitudes of 40° and 50° South, where towering waves are often encountered. And many a life on land also comes up against unprecedented storms during the fourth and fifth decades of life. Do you recognize any squally weather in these transitional seasons of your life?

- A clash of weather systems: if you follow the daily weather reports with any interest, you will often have noticed the instability that arises when, for example, a high and a low pressure band meet. It isn't too difficult to translate this kind of clash into the language of our own inner conflicts—clashes of loyalty, conflicts of desire, the eternal struggle between "what I want" and "what I ought," fomented by all the invisible currents that have formed our thinking patterns since before we could even speak.

- The kind of radar blackout that catches us unawares when we have failed to listen to the signs of the times. Small boats in high seas can experience radar blackout when they are caught in the trough between two mountainous waves. We too can find ourselves at a complete loss as to where we are or what we should do when circumstances overwhelm us. The storms that arise in families contending across the generation gap can often be traced back to a breakdown in communication like this. There is a widespread resistance to the idea that anything good could be coming out of the next generation, or, indeed, that anything good is to be expected of the generation that precedes us. It is hardly surprising that these attitudes lead to stormy relations.

- Refusal to go along with what our deepest heart knows to be the right course. The biblical story of Jonah spells out for us the kind of consequences we can expect if we persist in denying the wisdom of our heart's compass. Jonah knows very well that he should go to Nineveh, but fear seduces him into trying to run away from his true course. Such flight is useless. There is something about our destiny that very often brings us back, somehow or other, to the very place from which we were trying to run away. Difficult decisions, uneasy relationships, hard choices—they all have a tendency to keep coming back, perhaps in disguise, until we finally deal with them. Meanwhile, as we struggle, our inner seascape seems to become ever wilder.

The effects of these various storms can be far-reaching and destructive:

- They evoke our deepest fears: the fear of ceasing to exist, ceasing to have meaning or significance; the fear that creation itself may be meaningless; and the fear that even our relationships with those around us may be illusory and impermanent.

- They trap us in our isolation, convinced that we are alone in all we are feeling and experiencing, and that no one else has ever struggled in storms like these.

- They seduce us into reacting out of panic, with all our energy focused on the negative feelings rather than on attending to the cause of the storm.

- They can tempt us to give up our inner journey, and, like the children of Israel in the desert, to turn back to Egypt, preferring our former captivity and incompleteness to the challenges of a life on these unpredictable oceans.

Dealing with the storms

No! There are no answers. Indeed, I am always suspicious of those who claim to provide answers. The only answers that matter, that really help us to ride the storms and grow as a result of the experience, are the ones we discover for ourselves.

However, if seafaring can be a helpful metaphor for life, then the experience of those who go to sea might offer some clues about dealing with the storms. So it might be helpful to look at some of the real things that real sailors do when they find themselves in trouble on the waves.

Reflect

A few pieces of nautical wisdom are suggested below. See whether any of them speak to your own situation or offer practical guidance on how to deal with any storms that are around in your life.

- *Go higher, go deeper:* it is said that there is calmer water a mere ten feet below the trough of the highest waves. Pilots also report that flying conditions at high altitudes can be very much more stable than the turbulence found at lower altitudes. A very valuable way of dealing with our life's turbulence can be to make space regularly to be still, at a deeper (or a higher) level of awareness, in reflective prayer. New perspectives often emerge out of this kind of stillness, and the clamor of the immediate turmoil can give way to the deeper, more eternal rhythms and harmonies that alone will redirect our course.

- *Search for focus, for concentration, and clear vision:* the skipper of a boat in trouble will make sure that he has a point on deck from which the view ahead is clearest. He will look for an unrestricted view of all that is going on, both on the vessel, and at sea, and he will probably want to be alone, to concentrate deeply on the task in hand. Prayer gives us such a space—a space to be alone, and to focus in a more intensive way on everything that forms our circumstances, both in our immediate living, and in the larger context of the whole human journey with God.

- *Conserve energy:* on board ship, all unnecessary energy expenditure must be curtailed in times of storm, so that essential battery power is preserved for emergency purposes, such as radio contact and flashlight power. When the storms beset us, we do well to commit our limited energy reserves to seeking a clear vision, spending time in prayer, and focusing on what is most essential in our journeying. This may mean letting go of much inessential anxiety and unfruitful "busy-ness."

- *Use the bilge pumps:* high seas rapidly swamp the decks, the cargo, and everything else on board little boats. The storms of our life can do the same to us. If circumstances seem to be overwhelming you, and you feel you are drowning in them, see if there is anything you can do to pump away the surplus water. Much of what comes at us during the storms is not stuff that we need to take on board. Have another look at chapter 2, and see whether you can bale out some of the bilge water that you really don't need, and that may be threatening your life support systems. Sometimes, for example, it is both possible and necessary to respond to a problem with the acknowledgment that this is not, in fact, your problem.

- *Set manageable targets:* in the midst of a hurricane, the skipper of a small boat set on sailing round the world can feel utterly demoralized as she reflects on how many thousands of miles there are still to cover. It can be more helpful, in this situation, to focus on the next expected sighting of land, and take the journey in smaller stages. In our living, we too can be overwhelmed by the thought of everything we are trying to achieve in our little lives, and how impossible it all appears. The sense of impossibility is eased if we think simply about what we are doing today.

- *Add ballast to make weight:* a lightweight vessel can be tossed around mercilessly on a stormy sea. Sometimes it is necessary to add ballast (by taking on seawater into the hold in a controlled way), to add stability to the boat. A common human reaction to life's storms is the very opposite of this: we go off for a little "retail therapy," anesthetizing ourselves to the difficulties around us by moving into the realm of the trivial and the superficial, in order temporarily to forget the bigger questions. Sailing wisdom suggests that it might be better to add weight so that our boats lie deeper in the ocean. We might do this by turning, perhaps, to the wisdom of the past, by opening ourselves to the wisdom of creation in our parks and gardens, or by speaking in depth with a friend, rather than fleeing to the shopping malls.

- *Keep the distress channel clear:* remember channel 16, and the golden rule that it must never be clogged up by nonemergency conversations. When you are struggling, do you know the fastest route to God? What does it mean for you? If you go overboard, what helps you get back to safety? Who or what are your personal life-lines? Perhaps a tried and tested method of prayer, or a key piece of scripture, or a particular soul friend who will be there for you? Locate and name your channel 16 while the sea is calm, so that you can find it instantly when the storms break.

- *Make the most of any fine weather:* during any breaks in the storm, a wise sailor will take the opportunity to carry out essential maintenance—baling out, adjusting the sails, fixing the bilge pump, ensuring that the transmitter is in working order, and, most importantly, using the clear weather to check the navigation. Even the fiercest onslaught of spiritual desolation will eventually yield to fairer weather. During desolation, try to return, in your prayer, to periods of consolation when you could see the vision that is energizing you and urging you forward. The vision is still there, just as the sun doesn't stop shining simply because we can't see it through the clouds. Whenever there is a break in the storm, and you feel reconnected to the larger vision of your heart, take the opportunity to take your bearings, and to reconnect with the world around you, responding to its needs and allowing it to nourish you.

- *Tell stories:* the great maritime adventures in our history and literature always speak of the sailor's special gift for spinning yarns. Telling stories turns the darkest night into a place of companionship and even of laughter. We won't usually feel like telling stories or entertaining each other when the storms are battering our lives. But we all have a story to tell, and the sharing of our stories is one of the key ingredients of what it means to be a spiritual pilgrim. If things are grim, try listening to another person's story. (People are usually more than willing to share their stories if they find a willing listener.) And maybe tell yourself, or a friend, something of your own story. As we tell our stories (even to ourselves), we hear them in new ways, and we often see patterns emerging that reveal a meaning in the mystery.

- *Stay cheerful:* during his attempt to circumnavigate the globe alone in 1968, Robin Knox-Johnston devised a fail-safe recipe for cheering himself up on cold dark nights, while the southern gales buffeted his boat, the *Suhaili*. He made himself a drink of brandy, honey, hot water, sugar, and a lemon. Sailors traditionally carry casks of rum with them for the same purpose.

Reflect

What is your recipe for bucking yourself up when the chips are down? Is there perhaps a spiritual equivalent of Knox-Johnston's nightcap? Perhaps some brew that combines whatever gives you spirit, whatever gives you joy, whatever provides you with energy, and whatever adds the sharp tang to keep you alert? You might like to reflect on what these key ingredients might mean for you.

A little boat in deep waters

Very few of us ever expect the storms that overtake us in our lives. Most of us live in the illusion that things will, more or less, go our way and that creation will, on the whole, be kind to us. For some, this illusion is shattered at an early age, perhaps by sickness or disability,

113

abuse or abandonment. Some of us get a bit older before life lets us down. But sooner or later, the vast majority of human travelers hit storms for which they are wholly unprepared.

I was fascinated one day by a TV documentary about the salvaging of a boat that began as a very ordinary sailing barge, and found herself playing a crucial role in world history. Perhaps her story may engage in some way with your own?

The *Ena* was a Thames sailing barge, built around a hundred years ago when these sailing vessels plied up and down the Thames and around the south coast of Britain, sometimes even crossing to France, delivering raw materials for industry or removing London's waste to be dumped at sea. They were workhorses, constructed to sail shallow waters and carry heavy cargo. The *Ena* went about her lawful business for more than thirty years, and she might have gone on doing so for many years more, had not the fateful command been issued in 1940 to mobilize every boat, large or small, to sail across immediately to France to rescue the many thousands of British and allied troops stranded and cornered on the beaches of Dunkirk. The *Ena* was one of those "Little Ships." Suddenly she found herself engaged in a dangerous mission. She made the journey across the channel, along with the hundreds of other boats pressed into emergency service. But when she landed, her captain was forced to abandon her on the beach in the face of overwhelming enemy action and flee for his life. And there she might have stayed, tossing precariously in the waters off Dunkirk. Indeed, her owner could find no trace of her.

But it happened that the *Ena*'s fate was twinned with the destiny of one of the soldiers trapped on the beaches. As he reached the shoreline, he realized that he had, quite literally, missed the last boat home. The future looked grim, to say the least, as enemy fire pounded all around him. Until he noticed a hapless sailing barge bobbing out in the bay. He had never manned a ship in his life, but he rapidly gathered a few dozen stragglers and together they made their way out to the *Ena* and clambered aboard. A bomb, landing only a few feet away from the *Ena*'s bows, tossed her like a cork out of the water, but the sturdy barge was not deterred and the motley crew set sail, to arrive eventually at Margate. The *Ena* took her place proudly among the "Little Ships of Dunkirk" before returning to her routine duties until she was left to disintegrate in the mudflats of the Medway, her useful life apparently over.

Two ordinary lives. An old boat's and an old soldier's. And ours too! A brief blaze of action, and then back to the routine trudge again, until we eventually fall apart upon the sands of time. But the *Ena*'s story is not yet fully told—and neither are yours or mine! The TV program showed how the *Ena* is being salvaged in order to race again in the traditional barge race and to become a beloved home for her owner. But what was more important for me, in this little story, is the inspiration that the *Ena* can give us and the ways in which she tells us something of our own story—the story of how circumstances can change our weather overnight, and challenge us to face the unexpected in ways that bring life to others. The story of how there is no such thing as an "ordinary" life, for everything ordinary contains the seeds of the extraordinary. The story of how all life is being continually renewed, to become the cherished and eternal home of its Creator.

Monsters and mutineers

Not all the storms in our inner seas are caused by events beyond ourselves, and not all of them result in visibly stormy weather. The deep oceans of life, and of our own subconscious and unconscious minds, contain unfathomed mysteries, and often it is from these mysterious depths that the perils appear to arise. But unless you are a submarine or a shark, how can you know what may be lurking under the surface of your life's seas?

One thing that helps me in monster detection is to notice any evidence on the surface of invisible activity going on below the surface of my life. Just as a subaquatic presence will betray itself by an occasional ring of bubbles or a spurt of exhaled water, so my inner monsters will sometimes reveal their whereabouts, perhaps in the form of a sudden outburst of irrational or uncharacteristic behavior, an overreaction to a harmless remark or strong feelings that I can't account for. These little signs are often the traces of something powerful going on in a deeper layer of my psyche. They are invitations to have a look at these deeper issues.

Unfortunately, it is much easier to fire in haste and reflect at leisure when it comes to the monsters of the deep. When we sense something unresolved cruising in the dark waters of our minds and hearts, a snap (and unconscious) reaction is to take the harpoon to it before it can do any damage, a practice that psychologists would probably call repression. And if it isn't possible to get a direct hit, the next best thing is to hit out at the nearest visible target, and so some other unfortunate becomes the recipient of our irrational feelings. This, I believe, is what the psychologists might call transference. The wisdom of those who have dared to face their monsters is surprising: it urges us to befriend the shadow that lurks in the deeps. "Befriending" implies entering into some form of fruitful dialogue with this shadow, in the hope of addressing the deeper issues that it represents. Befriending the shadow is a topic that goes far beyond the scope of this book, but some further help may be found in the books listed in the Bibliography.

While the monsters are largely invisible and unconscious, the mutineer is usually very visibly on deck, challenging and questioning what is going on onboard ship, and especially challenging the competence of the skipper. The mutineer is driven by desperation, and eventually takes over the command of the ship for the greater good of all. The pirate, on the other hand, takes over the ship for his own benefit, and usually for nefarious ends.

Perhaps there has been piracy in your life? Maybe others have hijacked your energies and good will for their own purposes and left you feeling exploited? Or maybe there is some unacceptable oppression around for you? Sometimes stultifying, suffocating, or even abusive relationships can lead us to the brink of mutiny, even against our nearest and dearest. Sometimes an unscrupulous colleague in the workplace can make unjust demands upon us or seek to shape our lives in ways that we cannot accept. Or, most difficult of all, sometimes we find pirate activity going on inside ourselves, when one aspect of our inner self seems to be undermining our deeper dream. "I'm my own worst enemy," we may ruefully have to admit to ourselves. Such situations may justifiably cry out for mutiny, as we rightly reclaim our own integrity. If you find yourself in a place like this, take heart from the calm and simple takeover of the *Caine* in 1944: "Captain, I'm sorry, sir, you're a sick man. I am temporarily relieving you of this ship." Would that it were as easy to challenge the assumed authority of your boss or your partner, or even your lesser self, but sometimes mutiny can be the only way to remain true to yourself.

Shipwreck

A great-uncle of mine was third engineer on the *Titanic*. He had moved from Fraserburgh to Southampton to join the White Star line, and with all the engineering crew and nearly 1,500 others he died that April night in 1912 in the North Atlantic when the *Titanic* struck an iceberg on her maiden voyage. Thirty years later, his son, a merchant seaman on a North Atlantic convoy ship, lost his life as a result of enemy action. We discovered later, from naval records, that the convoy ship sank at almost exactly the same spot as the *Titanic*, 41°44'N, 50°24'W.

I come from a long line of seafarers, and so, perhaps, the possibility of disaster at sea is imprinted into my genes, and I have often reflected on how I would have reacted had I been on board the *Titanic* on that fateful night. These thoughts were particularly active during a period when I felt I was going through a personal shipwreck myself, and the story of the loss of the *Titanic* opened up some searching questions for me—questions I still haven't entirely resolved.

Reflect

You might like to join me in my reflections, carrying in your mind and heart any personal experiences that felt like shipwreck when you were going through them. Perhaps you are even in such a situation right now. . . .

The severity of the situation has become clear. The command has been issued to load the lifeboats: women and children first. First and second class passengers are guided to the boat deck. Steerage passengers are largely left to fend for themselves. A woman remonstrates with a crew member. She will not go until her jewels are released by the purser. She insists. She is immoveable. Within hours she will be saved, without her jewels, and the crewman who now stands coaxing her will drown. Another terrified passenger screams hysterically. She is afraid to make the jump from liner to lifeboat. The obvious and immediate fear still looms larger than the fear of the as yet unknown. A mother's ordered world is torn apart in the icy night. To save her children she must abandon her husband.

How many cogent reasons there are to be suspicious of rescue! I marvel at our amazing capacity to resist our own salvation, and the complications inherent in apparently simple choices. So easy to make judgments from this distance in time. How would I have reacted? Would my mind have believed the evidence of my eyes or the propaganda of unsinkability? Would I have scrambled for a place in the overcrowded lifeboats, which could in any case accommodate less than half of those on board? Would I have drunk myself into a stupor, as some did? Or worked myself into oblivion, like the ship's radio operator? Would I have despaired, panicked, jumped, or prayed?

The last lifeboat has been lowered. A honeymoon couple watch their last hope drift away into the night. An officer stops to speak to them, admiring their calm.

"Take my advice," he says, "don't wait until the last minute before you go overboard, or the suction as the ship sinks will drag you down, and you won't have a chance."

They acknowledge the advice gratefully. Out in one of the lifeboats, an altercation begins. Some of the women who are rowing want to return to take on more of their hapless fellow passengers. The navigator tries to stop them, saying that the little boat will be swamped by would-be survivors. Of course, he is right. And so are they.

Where would we be without common sense? What will we become without compassion? How much would I sacrifice, and for whom? Would I save myself at the expense of another? And what about that moment when the time is right to jump into the near-freezing waves, with only a life jacket between me and certain death? Should I jump, or stay with the ship? When it sinks it will suck me down with it. By then I must be far enough away from it. I ponder my own problems, my own ship, and wonder about its power to suck me down to destruction. The questions remain unanswered. I stand on the deck, nervously fingering my life jacket, afraid to stay, afraid to jump.

Meanwhile the radio operator keeps on clicking out his signals to a cold, dark, unresponsive world. Engineers keep on going through the motions of running an ocean liner, attending to routine tasks, more doggedly than ever in the face of despair. And the band keeps on playing. . . .

Because sometimes, when all light has been extinguished except the flickering flame of duty and habit, perhaps in the blank darkness of bereavement, the only response to disaster is to keep on doing what you think you ought to do, or what those you love and respect would expect and want you to do.

The death-throes of the unsinkable liner are over. The stars shine out in infinite beauty over the cold sea. The screams have given way to silence. Even in the lifeboats, many are dead, the rest stunned by exhaustion. The path to salvation is no triumphalist procession, but truly a via dolorosa. Not one has been saved by his or her own efforts, but by the hands, hearts, and sacrifice of others. Pride is inappropriate. Just gratitude. And there is no energy left even for that. A rocket flare is sighted a few miles away. The Carpathia has arrived to lift sevenhundred survivors from the sea.

How does it feel to lie on the deck, wrapped in a blanket, empty with shock? What humankind has so proudly put together, a straying iceberg, in a single gash, has put asunder. All that was valued—possessions, lifestyle, the illusion of security, the permanence of relationships—has gone forever into impenetrable depths. It is a time to look for new realities, for nothing will ever again be as it was before.

My own *Titanic* still lurched at a sick angle in the wild sea of my circumstances as they were then. I remember how I begged God to hover over my chaos, and I believe that in my darkness I heard a whisper of that creating Word—just a whisper: "I will bring a new order out of the chaos, but you may not easily recognize the new creation. Nothing can ever be the same again after you have come through these waters. The way through the waves will leave you so shocked and limp on the deck of my *Carpathia* that it will take time before you realize my new reality for you." It did take time. The process is still incomplete, and perhaps can never be completed in ways I can grasp in my own lifetime. But now I can say, with conviction, that the promise was true.

On the rocks with Paul

If the image of shipwreck is dominant for you, either now or in recent memory, you might find it helpful to join the Apostle Paul as he faces an unwanted and ill-fated voyage (described in Acts 27).

Paul is a prisoner. You could call him a "prisoner of conscience." His desire to spread the Good News has brought him right into the heart of the storms of opposition. All appeals to people's deeper longings for God have failed. He finds himself put unceremoniously on board a ship: a captive, with no control over his own destiny, given over into the power of wind, weather, and the will of other people and guarded by soldiers. We join him as the ship is about to set sail.

In what ways do you feel like a prisoner? What parts of your own life feel out of your control or at the mercy of circumstances you cannot change? Have your own attempts to share your faith ever met real opposition?

At first things don't go too badly at all. The voyage goes to plan. There is even an interlude in one port where he is allowed to spend time with friends who look after him and maybe spoil him a bit.

Remember times and people who have given you respite when you needed it. Thank God for them in your prayer.

But soon the winds begin to blow against the boat, with its cargo of 276 people. The crew try to search out the most sheltered route, hugging the coastline, struggling on against the wind from one small port to the next. Sometimes the direction of the wind carves a line straight across all their planning. Faced with an impasse, they have to continually rethink their journey. Until at last they reach a place called "Safe Harbors" (or "Fair Havens" in some accounts), where they drop anchor to ride out the storms.

Have there been times in your own journey of faith when you felt threatened, tried to find a safer way to travel, or when something blocked your best intentions. Where, and with whom, have you experienced the security of a safe haven?

This is fine while it lasts, but all the while valuable time is being lost. By now it is well on in the year, nearly the time of the autumn equinox—a notoriously bad time for weather. There is a debate about what to do: to carry on regardless and take their chances, or to abandon the journey. Paul points out to them that to sail on is to court disaster. Not only will they lose their cargo, and their boat, but quite probably 276 lives as well. There is sense in what he says. They know that. But there are other voices louder than his: the voice of profit, for example, reminding them that the voyage is about making money for the boat's owners; the voice of pride, suggesting that they are stronger than all the storms; and the voice of fear, making them cringe at what account they will have to give of themselves to their employers back on land if they abort the journey. These other voices are louder than the wind. And the decision is taken to sail on.

Our decisions are often loaded in many different directions. Remember any important decision you may be facing. What factors are at work? Notice the pull of the different voices: perhaps fear or pride, stubbornness, profit, status. Notice the pull within you that, deep down, really knows which is the better, wiser, or more loving thing to do.

As if to encourage them in their folly, a soft wind from the south begins to blow. Heartened by this, they weigh anchor and off they sail. But again, not long out of harbor, a north-easterly wind blows up. Strong in their self-assurance, the sailors try to keep the ship headed straight into the wind. A hopeless cause! Soon they have to abandon the attempt, and from then on the wind just carries them wherever it will. They have no choice but to let themselves be carried. They have become prisoners of circumstance no less than Paul, their "on-board captive." Occasionally there might be a lull, but it only offers them a false sense of security before reality reasserts itself.

When have you had to give up and let yourself be driven by the winds? Remember any times like that now in your prayer. Don't make any judgments. Just let God hold both you, and the storms, and the despair. God is bigger than all of it.

Things are looking serious. It is time to trim the lifeboat and secure it, so that at least it won't get swept overboard. It isn't only the force of the storm they have to fear, but the very real chance of being swept onto sandbanks. They take down the sail and abandon themselves completely to the power of the wind.

The next day there is no improvement. Now the next stage of the struggle begins. It is time to start jettisoning some of the cargo. First the merchandise is thrown overboard. The hope of profit is abandoned because the need to cling to life is so much stronger. Another day passes, and the ship's equipment is hurled overboard. Whatever aids to navigation they have are less important to them now than the raw desire to survive. Finally, the heavens themselves close down on them. For days on end they can see neither sun nor stars. Blindly they are swept through the seas like driftwood on the angry breath of the storm. They give up all hope of being saved.

Imagine yourself on the boat of your own life's journey. The storms are strengthening. Your only hope of coming through is to throw unnecessary baggage overboard. What will you let go of?

Life on board is grim. Food is being severely rationed, and everyone is close to starvation and despair. It is then that Paul has a dream! The next morning he gathers them round and makes them a promise that sounds like pure fantasy:

"I warned you," he reminds them, "when we first set out that this was going to be a hiding to nothing. If you'd listened to me then, we could have avoided all this loss and grief. But now that we are in the thick of it, I have good news for us all. I had a dream last night. The God whom I love and serve came to me in this dream and assured me that not one of you will be lost, though the ship itself will be destroyed. I trust the promise of my God. We will be marooned, but not destroyed. The God who created us will save us."

What dreams (sleeping or conscious) have kept you going through the worst times of your life? In what personal ways has God made himself known to you when you most needed him? Just remember those dreams, those times now, and express your thanks to him in your prayer.

While all this is going on, a little plot is hatching among some of the sailors. They know better than Paul, they think, about the outcome of this ill-fated journey. They know better than Paul's God. It is about midnight on the following night. The sailors have a feeling that they are not too far from land. They take depth soundings. First forty meters. Then thirty. Their hunch seems to be right. Quietly, like conspirators, they drop anchor at the stern and let themselves down into the lifeboat, pretending that they are going to drop further anchors around the bows of the boat. It is Paul, who blows this little plan right out of the water!

"If they go," he warns the guards and ship's officers, "there is no hope of us being saved. God's promise is for all of us, and it depends on us remaining together, united in our trust in him." So the officers cut the ropes that

are securing the lifeboat and let it go, in a gesture of trust that it will not, after all, be needed.

Have you ever been tempted to save yourself at the expense of someone else's good? Again, don't judge yourself, but just let the memory be there, in God's loving, accepting hands.

Daybreak comes, and Paul urges the people to have something to eat.

"You haven't eaten anything for two weeks," he reminds them. "If we are really ready to trust God's promise, we don't need to keep rationing the food like this. Come and eat. Strengthen yourselves. You need nourishment if you are going to survive." And Paul takes some bread in his hands, gives thanks to God for it, breaks it, and begins to eat it. At this they all take heart and help themselves to some of the bread. When they have eaten their fill, they throw the surplus grain overboard to lighten the ship even further.

Sometimes we hoard our treasure for a rainy day, but fail to use it when that rainy day actually happens. Is there any treasure that you are hoarding like this in your own life? Can you take it out now, in your prayer, bring it to God, and ask him what he actually wants you to do with it? Can you share it, if he asks you to, with those around you—those who are "in the same boat"?

When the next day dawns there is, indeed, land in sight. They don't know where they are, but they can see a kind of bay with a beach. The plan is to run the boat up against this beach if they can. They cut the anchors, leaving them behind in the sea, hoist the sail and head for the beach. But it is not to be. Cross-currents force the boat into a sandbank, and it begins to break up.

A panic ensues. The soldiers guarding the prisoners take a decision to kill them all in case they manage to swim to shore and escape. But the officer guarding Paul is absolutely determined to bring him to justice, and he refuses to let the prisoners be killed. Instead he gives the order for everyone who can swim to jump overboard and get to land, while the others are to cling to planks and bits of wreckage, and try to get to shore that way. And so it comes to be that all 276 of them are saved.

All are saved. All come through the worst that life has been able to throw at them, and they are cast on the beach of God's all-forgiving love. Spend a few moments on that beach, expressing your feelings in the silence of your prayer, to the God who has cared for you all through the storm. This is the God who asks you to trust him for all that is still to come.

Who shot the albatross?

In his narrative ballad "The Rime of the Ancient Mariner," Samuel Taylor Coleridge explores a powerful image of the human journey as a sea voyage, exposed to every kind of hazard and hardship, but also underpinned and energized by a greater presence that remains indestructible. In particular, he has immortalized the image of the albatross—the great white solitary bird who often accompanies seagoing craft during their voyages.

In Coleridge's poem, the voyage begins in relative calm. The boat sets sail in good heart but is soon blown by storm winds into polar regions and hostile weather. At this point the albatross flies alongside the boat, apparently out of nowhere, and with a benign presence that seems almost to come from beyond itself. The companionship of the albatross turns out to be a blessing upon the voyage. Under the power of this silent blessing, the helmsman is able to steer the craft through the ice floes, and a strong and favorable southerly wind springs up. In all weathers, through sunshine and fog, clear days and fear-filled nights, the bird follows faithfully.

And then, for no apparent reason, the ancient mariner shoots the albatross!

The repercussions begin at once. The fair winds change. The other mariners turn on the killer of the bird with their reproaches:

> Ah wretch! said they, the bird to slay,
> That made the wind to blow.

From then on the voyage is doomed. Fierce gales give way to motionless heat and unbearable thirst. The desperate crew hang the body of the dead albatross around the ancient mariner's neck, as a sign that he is the cause of the curse that has come upon them. Eventually all die, except the accursed mariner who has shot the bird, and who now lives on amid the bodies of his dead comrades on the deck, still staring their reproach at him from sightless eyes. He enters his own personal purgatory, and only when he has faced the depths of his own wrongdoing does the curse begin to lift.

This story is, of course, a powerful Christian allegory. Perhaps its power is even stronger today, in the so-called "new age," because of what it reveals of the deep interrelationship and interdependence of all creation. The albatross is a symbol of these sacred connections. When we break them for our personal gain or satisfaction, we bring the curse of disconnection upon ourselves, and we are cast out of the orbit of our original wholeness. We are not told why the mariner shoots the albatross. Perhaps it was for food. Perhaps it was just on a whim, to demonstrate his marksmanship. What we do know is that, collectively and individually, we too have the blood of the albatross on our hands. We have slaughtered the created world for our own ends and in the fulfillment of our own perceived needs. As a result we have pitched our planet into the storms and droughts, the plagues and famines that we read about every day in our newspapers (which are themselves the products of massacred rain forests). Like the gaze of the dead crew on the stricken boat, our TV screens beam back to us the reproachful faces of those whose lives are sacrificed in the two-thirds world, so that we may enjoy the luxuries of a consumer society. Coleridge's poem was more prophetic than he could have guessed.

Many of us, as Christians, wear a cross or crucifix around our necks, just as the ancient mariner wore the body of the albatross. Can this story give us any further clues as to how we might be freed of the curse we carry, and the shadow we cast across the stricken earth? For the guilty mariner, the curse begins to lift when the focus of his attention starts to move away from his own suffering and guilt and toward the presence of a larger creation, and its Creator. When he begins to pray, the dead bird falls from his neck and sinks back into the sea. The process of healing and renewal has begun. The reweaving of sacred connections becomes a possibility. For us, this might be the challenge to recognize and cherish the unique life within every part of creation, and to work to ensure that the universal right to life and the means of living is assured to all.

We might also ask ourselves how we respond to the changing circumstances of life. How often, in all cultures, but perhaps most damagingly and obviously in our Western capitalist culture, do we react to our problems either by hurling money at them, or by hurling weapons at them? The mariner shot the albatross. Who are our albatrosses today? A glance at the newspaper will name some of them for you! Yet the mariner's shot brought curse, not gain, and we don't need to look far to discover the same pattern in our own political and social responses to our problems. Our firepower, whether it takes the form of the dollar or the bomb, always brings curse, never gain.

Consider, by contrast, the power of the albatross itself. It sweeps the skies with its vast wingspan. It rides the thermals, sinking and rising with the air currents, flowing with the winds, responding to the elements, not fighting against them, faithfully accompanying the tiny human craft tossing on the waves below. As long as the benign interrelationship between the boat and the bird remains, the worst that the sea can do has no permanent power over the sailors and their boat. Once it is broken, however, the human voyager has lost the inner compass, the heart-knowledge of that deep relatedness that once kept the boat sound and the course sure. Ultimately, the power of the bird (a potent image, for Christians, of the Holy Spirit) is indestructible, but separated from it, the boat will sink. Ultimately, all the firepower that the world can muster is not capable of pushing a single crocus through the frozen winter soil. So is this really where we want to invest our energies? Which kind of power do we choose: the silent, sustaining power of God, or the reactive, destructive force of our own little ego-world?

The image of the albatross connects us to something archetypal in the human psyche which we disregard at our extreme peril. There is a knowledge deep in the human heart, I believe, that knows (albeit unconsciously) that benign presence that always accompanies our voyaging and will bless us if we nourish it and remain in right relationship with it. To this day, sailors will never kill an albatross. What does this image mean for you?

Across the water

The "albatross" sometimes comes to us on silent wings when we least expect it. The stormiest waters can be the very place that is leading us to deeper peace. As we move beyond the storms, let us take a few moments to join a group of struggling seafarers on the Sea of Galilee (as described in Matthew 14:22–33):

It had been an amazing day. The crowds had flocked to the hillside in their thousands to hear this man, Jesus, speak to them about the reality of God in their ordinary, everyday lives. Without anyone realizing how fast time was passing, the evening hour had come. People were hungry, but no one wanted to leave the teacher's side. A few packed lunches were brought out and shared around, and somehow or other everyone received enough to eat. It was a miracle, they thought. Surely this man was someone special!

His small group of close friends gathered round him at dusk as the last few people disappeared off home into the darkening valley. Like him, they were exhausted after the day's events. But Jesus didn't seem to notice their tiredness. Instead, he told them to get into a boat and cross to the other side of the Sea of Galilee, while he himself went up to the hills to pray.

The night deepened. Jesus was way off up in the hills, and the boat was quite a way out into the lake. A storm blew up. The wind was against them. They were struggling to keep going and there were those amongst them who were feeling resentful. "Why did he send us out alone on a night like this, when the winds are against us?"

We might echo their protest as we reflect on some of our own circumstances:

"Why has he sent me out into this situation all alone, when there is so much coming at me and he must know I can't handle it alone?"

They battled on, rowing against the wind, and beginning to fear for their lives. The storms on the Sea of Galilee could be vicious. They all knew that. It might be far from the open sea, but it had its own weather systems, and it took both courage and skill to venture across it in stormy conditions.

They struggled on until the small hours of the morning, and it was then that they saw someone gliding toward them, across the water. At first they were terrified. A ghost, they thought! Some supernatural presence haunting their exhausted minds. They screamed in fear. But the figure called out to them from the distance:

"Don't be afraid. It's me!"

Peter recognized the voice at once:

"If it's really you, Lord, and not some figment of our imagination, then call me to come to you, across the water."

And the word echoed back through the howling of the gale:

"Come!"

Peter trusted it. There was something here more powerful than the storms that surrounded him. He clambered over the side of the boat and began to walk across the water to the Lord, until his human survival instinct took over again and he became aware of the might of the waves pounding all around him and the winds shrieking through the night air. He began to sink.

"Lord, save me!" he called out in his panic.

But even before the cry for help was uttered, Jesus was there, holding him and drawing him gently out of the water.

"Why didn't you trust the evidence of your heart?" he asked. "You could have safely trusted me! My peace really is stronger than your storms." He said it in love, and together they climbed back into the boat and sank down into the bows, overwhelmed by their experience. And at once the storm abated.

Allow yourself, in your imagination, to join those friends on the waters of Galilee. What do the storms mean for you, right now? Are the winds against you? Where is the Lord in all this? Let him speak his word to you: "Come!" How do you want to react?

Often we have to cross a threshold of trust, if we are to deepen our relationship with God. We have to let go of our old understanding of what makes us "secure," in order to discover a new layer of solid ground in God. We sometimes have to step over the limits set by our common sense and human judgment to discover the potential that lies beyond what we thought was possible. Such insight and growth usually comes out of the stormy times of our lives rather than in the smooth stretches, and the encouragement to make such leaps of faith seems to be given silently and in the very depths of our darkness. Paradoxically, we hear that silent assurance in the midst of the storm, urging us to venture further, across the water.

CHAPTER

Going Nowhere

Imagine, if you will, two boats. One is a smart, sophisticated sloop called *Napoleon Solo*, the other a small inflatable raft called *Rubber Ducky*. *Napoleon Solo* was all set for a stunning voyage. *Rubber Ducky* came supplied with nothing more promising than a forty-day guarantee! But *Napoleon Solo* sank, leaving her skipper to survive as best he might in a hostile Atlantic aboard *Rubber Ducky*. Steven Callahan describes his experience in his book *Adrift*—the story of seventy-six days lost at sea in a raft guaranteed only for forty of them!

Perhaps everyone who ever embarks on what we call "the spiritual journey" experiences how it feels to be drifting on a personal equivalent of *Rubber Ducky*. Callahan's story is a reflection of all our stories. We set sail with grand plans for a stunning voyage in our own version of *Napoleon Solo*, only to find ourselves, at least from time to time, hopelessly adrift on a *Rubber Ducky* life-raft, hoping that we might arrive somewhere, somehow, before our guarantee runs out! The good news is that we may learn more about who we are and what we are about in the *Rubber Ducky* of our experience than we do in our *Napoleon Solo*.

In this chapter we will explore something of that experience of being adrift, out of control of our journey, or quite simply stuck in a deep rut along the way. A friend told me she had been walking across the fields one day in her sturdy wellies and rainproof jacket when she quite literally got stuck in the mud! The only way out was to extricate herself from her wellies, just before the mud came over their rims, and make a leap of faith on to a nearby tussock of grass. The incident rings loud bells in my own experience—and perhaps in yours too? We may feel that we are doing our level best to make this journey with God, and we are trying to do all the right things, but then we find ourselves wading through treacle, stuck in the mud, adrift on

Rubber Ducky, and we wonder what we have done wrong and how we are ever going to retrieve ourselves and get going again.

A painted ship upon a painted ocean

This kind of experience may take many forms. In "The Rime of the Ancient Mariner," Coleridge describes it in these words:

> Day after day, day after day,
> We stuck, nor breath nor motion,
> As idle as a painted ship
> Upon a painted ocean.

Steven Callahan puts it rather differently:

> Each day seems longer . . . We sit like a period in a book of blank pages.

If you find yourself in such a place, if you are feeling like a lonely full stop in the middle of a blank page, it may be helpful to begin by looking at just what kind of impasse it is. Let's explore a few of the most common possibilities. . . .

- *Is the boat unseaworthy?* The most vigorous voyager will be stopped in her tracks if illness or injury intervenes. One of the most surprising things about us human beings is that we see sickness and death all around us, on a daily basis, but never believe such things will happen to us. This, at least, is true of those with an incurably optimistic mind-set (others, of course, always expect the worst, and are seldom disappointed!). Yet the fact is that the human mind and body are both miraculous and fragile. It can happen from one day to the next, or even from one moment to the next, that our solid certainties are shaken and destroyed, and we have to deal with an experience of helplessness for which our education and upbringing have never prepared us. A broken boat will not make much headway. It may, at best, limp back to dry dock, there to submit to whatever needs to be done to make it whole again. If this is where you are, it may be time to look for your life-raft.

- *Are you about to run out of fuel or stores?* The little red marker registers danger. I am running dangerously low on fuel, but surely if I watch my speed, I might just make it home. . . . How often I have lived like that in my spiritual journeying! I see all the signs. Those warning indicators of impending burnout. But I have to do this one more thing, prepare this one more talk, write those letters, clean the house, prepare myself for the next meeting, finish the next project, get my children through their exams. . . . What am I trying to prove, I wonder? And who am I trying to prove it to? Then out of the blue, the energy indicator drops to zero, and the car grinds to a halt on the motorway. The boat is becalmed, with not a flutter of wind in her sails. I am going nowhere, in spite of my best intentions. I need refueling, and that isn't always as easy to arrange as it sounds.

- *Have you run aground?* Many a seagoing boat has run aground by hugging the coastline for too long and drifting into too shallow waters. Remember that call, in chapter 3, to "put out into deeper waters." Might it be that your boat is longing for more depth, and more space to sail? Is the routine life along the coastline becoming stale for you, though you feel you need its safety and its comfortable familiarity? To put out into deeper water may be a scary prospect; it may also be the one thing necessary right now to prevent a dangerous "bottoming out." Or perhaps you have run aground on a submerged rock or sandbank that the charts never told you about? If so, take the time to discover what that submerged presence is about. It may be calling for your attention, and grounding you upon itself until you do give it that needful attention that will ultimately be healing and life-giving, even though it may be something you are trying not to look at.

- *Have you lost your vision or your sense of direction?* It sounds so final, and terrible. To lose our Christian vision is something most of us would see as some kind of profound failure, or "sin," yet, if we are honest, there are times in our journeying when we don't know where we are going because we simply can't see. It may be the depths of a "dark night of the soul" that afflict us, or it may be the thick fogs of our own doubts and questions. A common, and often helpful response to this plight is to keep on going through the motions, because we sense intuitively that it would be unwise to change a familiar course at such a time. Yet we may also wonder whether perhaps we are not facing the real questions underneath the fog. We may even step up the speed of our boat in order to get through the darkness faster, when perhaps what we need to do is to become still and listen to the movements deep within our own hearts. A sailor would warn us, in these circumstances, not to thrash around or try to steer "blind," but to let the boat show the way. "A boat at anchor," Richard Bode tells us in *First You Have to Row a Little Boat*, "like a gull on a post, is a weather vane; it points into the wind." So it may be important, when you are feeling lost and blindly adrift, to perch on the post for a while like the gull and listen to the wind. It might be a call to rest trustfully in "the cloud of unknowing," which all mystics through the ages have recognized as one of the ways in which God's mystery can enfold us.

- *Are you stranded?* We can feel, especially in our later years, that we have been left "high and dry" by the ebbing tides of life. Everything rushes on without us, and we need our grandchildren to show us how to work the video. We begin to wonder what our living has all been about, and this can bring us to a sorrowful halt on the beach, with little motivation for voyaging any further. Or perhaps circumstances have swept the ocean away from under us, through redundancy or bereavement or the breakdown of a significant relationship. It feels as though everything that once gave us life and buoyancy has drained away. Hope has turned into despair. Or we may have been caught out by an incoming tide, some unexpected turn of events, or some new season of our living that has come upon us more precipitately than we had anticipated. The next port that we had set our sights on is no longer accessible, and we have to change our plans, maybe radically. So, what are the tides doing to you right now? And how do you feel about them?

- *Are you going round in circles?* Few things are more frustrating than trying to find your way in unknown terrain, walking for what seems like several miles, only to come, once more, upon some landmark you noticed a couple of hours ago. All that energy expended, just to bring you back to where you began! We can meet these feelings at the end of a normal day. All that energy expended, and nothing seems to have been achieved. Tomorrow we will start over again exactly where we started this morning, and what is the point of it all? It is all too common to feel trapped in our own routine. How do we move on in our voyaging when we are stuck in a place like this?

- *Are you ice-bound?* In his book *Shackleton's Boat Journey*, F. A. Worsley, captain of the *Endurance*, describes his experience of how "the sea, breaking over the boats, froze in great masses on bows and sterns." Sometimes our own seas seem to do that, and we become solidly locked in the ice floes of our fears or our prejudices. Fears that tell us not to risk love, lest we be hurt or rejected, or to avoid expressing ourselves, in case we make ourselves into objects of ridicule. Prejudices that keep the doors firmly locked against experiences or relationships that might be full of gifts for us if only we were not afraid to be exposed to them. The shape and texture of the ice floes are many and varied, but they all have the same effect. They hold us in a frozen place and block our growth. Yet even frozen ground can be the cradle of new life, as every crocus and every snowdrop will confirm.

- *Is the "crew" being difficult?* Sometimes the boat gets stuck because either we ourselves, or those we are trying to work with, come up against an attitude problem. Maybe the crew is getting fed up and losing confidence in the captaincy of the boat, or maybe there is disunity among them. If several people are trying to steer, each in their own direction, the result is not likely to be progress. On the other hand, if the direction is being unilaterally imposed, the resulting lack of motivation of the crew can bring the boat to a halt. A sense of being stuck in this kind of place may be a call to explore new channels of communication or to question old ways of doing things that are no longer working.

- *Is the ocean deserted?* On the other hand, there may simply be no "crew," no accompanying fleet, no sign of any other life at all upon the ocean. Elderly people sometimes describe their lives in these terms, perhaps when all their friends have died and their families may be far away. Other lonely voyagers include those who feel marginalized, either by society or by the church or both, maybe because they fail to conform in some way, or they feel they have failed, or they are at the end of their physical and spiritual resources and don't feel they "belong" anywhere. Life, for such people, can very easily begin to feel like a journey that is going nowhere.

- *"Rubbish days"*: A friend of mine talks about days like this, and I think many of us could identify with the feeling, that may just last a day or two, or may be chronic, of being stuck in a place where nothing really works out as we would wish, or where perhaps failing health frustrates our physical capabilities and steals our energy, or days when, quite frankly, we don't rightly know what to do with ourselves. My friend is a contemplative person, and she has learned how to stop fighting her "rubbish days" and simply be content to be still within the frustrations and at peace about the fact of apparently going nowhere.

Whatever form our "feeling stuck" may take, it has the effect of becalming us. We feel helpless in a kind of restless stillness and any activity on our own part seems pointless. We can't fight a becalming in the way we have learned to fight the storms. It forces us into a waiting time—waiting for that first slight breath of breeze, that first almost imperceptible thaw in the ice, or the first tiny glimmer of light through the fog or the dark night—scanning the horizon for a sign of change that might lift us beyond the stagnation or free us from the paralysis that grips us. Such times can go on and on, perhaps for years, as we may know to our cost. Do they mean that we have been abandoned by God? The experience of spiritual voyagers through the ages would seem to say a resounding "No!" God is still there, in the very heart of the experience, in the fog that blankets us and the ice that freezes us into immobility. "Blessed are those who have not seen, but have believed," Jesus tells us, and perhaps the people who keep on living a faithful life of prayer in spite of feeling stuck are the real saints among us.

Reflect

Take the time to reflect on what is causing any becalming in your own life at present, before we move on to look at some ways, not only of surviving, but of growing through these times in our lives. Becalming can be a catalyst for change.

Survival kit

The chances are that your *Rubber Ducky* won't have overmuch space for all you might think you need to survive a season of drifting. You are going to have to think small. What are you going to pack in your survival kit to see you through a period of being lost, or grounded, blind, or simply in the doldrums? Here are a few suggestions:

- some means of getting drinking water

- some means of obtaining food

- some means of attracting attention or calling for help

- some lateral thinking

- an attitude of focused awareness

What might these things mean for us on our spiritual journey? How can we help ourselves to reconnect with our deeper source when we are feeling stranded in the middle of what feels like a spiritual wasteland?

Prayer: turning experience into wisdom

Sailors marooned in the doldrums, or ice-bound, or adrift without any obvious means of survival, turn their attention first to the problem of obtaining fresh drinking water. There are various means of doing this. One is to collect rain water. Another is to distil seawater to make it fit to drink. In our spiritual life, prayer can provide us with the fresh spring water of God's presence. That presence is, of course, always there, but prayer makes us aware of it and gives it access to our hearts and lives. It distils a fragment of the cloud of God's mystery into water that gives us life. Prayer can be something that is quite simply given, like rainwater that soaks into our driest experience and opens it up to new life. When we are becalmed, the reserves of drinking water, in the form of prescribed or set prayers that we may have drawn on in the past, may have run out, and we are challenged to discover ways of letting our own experience become the raw material of our prayer.

Prayer can be the means of taking the salty, sometimes corrosive or destructive experience of our everyday life and distilling it into something fresh and life-giving. Just as our streams and rivers flow down to the sea carrying all the residue of life's toil and struggle, and the seawater evaporates into the clouds to fall once again as fresh rain upon the hills, so prayer can flow through our days, carrying the detritus of our hopes and dreams into the waiting ocean of God's love. There God recycles our experience, showing us what is life-giving and to be fostered, and what is destructive to us and to be set aside. As our prayers "rise" to God, carrying our ordinary experience in their clouds, they are distilled into the fresh water of new hope and new direction. And this fresh water falls upon us and upon our circumstances, bringing new growth to our hearts and cleansing and refreshing the channels of our personal experience.

Reflect

One practical way to "collect" the fresh water in prayer is to foster the habit of noticing God's presence and action in everyday things, in the people around us and the ordinary events and encounters that happen to us, and to notice any ways in which God has rewoven the brokenness of our experience into new designs for fuller living. When you feel you are adrift, especially, try taking a little time each day to ask yourself: "What has awakened new life, fresh energy, in me today? What has caught my attention and reminded

me that I and my life-raft are not the center of the universe?
What has made me rejoice, or feel compassion, or a desire to
speak out for justice? What has made me feel loved today?"
Where love is, there is God. You may find at the end of the
day that you have collected more living water than you
expected and that God has recycled the apparent "waste" of
the past into pure water for the future.

Finding soul food

After the problem of fresh water, the next most important thing
for survival is the food that gives us the energy to keep going. When
we find ourselves stuck, how might we find the necessary nourishment? Those who come adrift at sea don't have an easy task in this
respect, as any of their stories will confirm. They may have to learn to
fish, and to improvise the means to catch the fish, and they will also
need to think about how to keep their food in a usable condition, how
to make it last, and how to use it wisely so that they get what their
bodies need in some kind of balanced diet.

"Soul food" may well be in short supply when you are feeling
spiritually adrift or in the doldrums. And then again, some unexpected tidbit may come your way when you least expect it.

Steven Callahan describes how he had to learn to fish from aboard
his *Rubber Ducky*, and the sheer struggle it was to catch something he
could eat. But he also comments that occasionally there would be
an unexpected feast. "This is a strange prison," he writes, "in which
I am slowly starved but occasionally thrown a twenty-pound filet
mignon."

It may be helpful to reflect on what, exactly, does give you spiritual nourishment, and how you can find more of it as you drift. It may
take a determined effort to do so, but begin where you are and ask
yourself whether any of these things, for example, might take you
deeper into the core of your being, and open up fresh "food supplies"
for you in your need:

- A time spent simply being in the created world,
  knowing yourself to be a unique and integral part

of that creation, without trying to work anything out or solve any problems.

- A book that has inspired you in the past—maybe poetry, or something by an author who is on your wavelength, or a novel that seems to have some depth and appeal for you.

- Some music that nourishes you in your depths, or a theater visit or concert that will open up new thought patterns for you, or refresh old memories of times when you felt closer to God.

- A journey to a place you love, or a place you have never been before, or maybe a visit to a friend you can really talk to.

I suggest these things because, above all, they are pleasurable, as well as being nourishing and having the potential to draw us back to God at the core of our being. The food we need when we are "down and out" needs to be even more attractively served than usual to tempt our jaded palate. Whatever you choose, by way of a food supply, do let it be something that gives you appetite; if it doesn't, you will probably give up half way through the meal.

And don't forget to be mindful of those unexpected feasts that occasionally land on the deck of *Rubber Ducky*. They can all too easily be missed, because we weren't expecting food from that quarter. What, in the past, has given you surprise nourishment? Can you trust that it will be so again in the future, and are you open to whatever surprising packaging such a feast may be wrapped in?

Calling for help

Very few of us can get ourselves beyond an impasse like this without help. Perhaps that is one of the gifts of such experience, that it forces us to recognize our interdependence on each other, and our total dependence on God. Yet our instinct when we find ourselves in the doldrums may be to curl up and give up. A kind of spiritual hypothermia sets in, and all we want to do is fall asleep and let the world get on with its own doings. We all know that to fall asleep when you are lost, either in the mountains or at sea, is the worst possible strategy. Such a sleep will usually be the victim's last. But it demands a great effort of will to summon the energy to call for help—to set off that flare that may attract attention—to call up channel 16 with your MAYDAY message. I was reminded by a sailor friend that MAYDAY derives from the French *m'aider*—"Help me!" Somehow it feels more personal and less demanding to whisper "m'aider" in the ear of a friend than to break the glass and set the emergency services in motion, and often this is all that is needed.

Reflect

So who will you call upon in your need? Who are your first lines of support in the spiritual journey? And are you someone else's first line of support? How do you respond to the possibility of such relationships? Our desperate cry to God when we are in need often translates into all these lesser cries to each other, and God most often responds to our cries through the ministry of another.

Getting a tow

The kind of friendship that will respond to a m'aider call may prove to be the companionship that takes on the quality of soul friendship—that sacred relationship between two pilgrims who choose to walk alongside each other through a particular stage of the journey. Do you have a soul friend? Do you have someone in your life who can and will give you a tow if you need it for a while? It may be someone who will lead you gently to the place you are longing to be, but dare not approach; someone who will carry you in prayer and hold the hope for you while you are too lost and helpless to pray for yourself.

Or it may be someone like the man in a story I once heard. A young lad was cycling, and had to make a very long journey on the day in question. His bike was loaded up with his baggage, and he was suffering from some kind of stomach upset, and hadn't been able to sleep the night before. The way was long and hilly, and the weather was oppressive. He struggled up a hill, feeling nauseous and close to despair. Then, out of the blue, another cyclist came up behind him, and greeted him as he made to overtake. Seeing that the first boy was struggling, he said "Would you like me to stay alongside for a while, and be a pacemaker?" and so the two of them plodded on. The second boy matched his pace to that of the first. They made slow, but steady progress. After a while the second boy suggested they might stop for a cup of tea, so they shared a small oasis of refreshment together before carrying on. The day drew on, and the second boy reached his own turn-off point, but he offered to make a detour, to go the extra few miles, to make sure that the first boy was well on his way again before they parted.

This (true) story shows how a tow can come along when we live with an awareness of each other's needs and are willing to respond to them in love, even if it slows us down or takes us out of our way. So, be open to those who may be offering you this kind of supportive companionship, and, likewise, to those who may be needing it from you.

Lateral thinking

The certainties and the skills we have known when we were sailing under full steam seem to disappear into the ether when we are drifting aimlessly in sluggish waters. We may have won the angling championships year after year, but out here on the *Rubber Ducky*, we don't have any of the kit, and we hardly know where to begin. We may be contenders for the Spirituality Olympics when things are going well, but when the winds fail and the sea is like glass, the old forms of prayer seem to trickle away into the salty wastes, leaving no trace of consolation in their wake.

Innovation is called for! New ways of praying may be helpful. Which new ways you might try depends a lot on the nature of the dry season you are in. It may be a genuine "dark night experience," in which case the new way of prayer might be simply to be there, waiting on God, doing nothing, expecting nothing, and simply trusting that in the depths, below the dry exterior, God's mystery is working its power at levels deeper than mind or imagination can fathom. If prayer is feeling dry and pointless for you, yet you nevertheless feel a desire to stay with it, this might be a dark night that is, in itself, leading you closer to God, so don't be tempted to walk away from it.

On the other hand, if you have a sense of staleness and stagnation, a feeling that you are getting pot-bound and needing fresh soil and more space to grow, then maybe it's time to experiment with ways of prayer you haven't used before. If you are used to vocal or set prayer, try a quieter form of reflective prayer, maybe using a passage of scripture as a focus. If you feel your prayer life and your real life are disconnected, maybe try engaging with Gospel scenes as though you were actually there, and notice any points of connection between what you are praying and what is actually going on in your life. If intercession has turned into a routine shopping list, try looking sideways at what it is you truly, deeply desire, underneath the layer of the things you are asking for, or try to enter imaginatively into the life of the person you are praying for—it may be that the answer to your prayers for that person is something God is asking you to deliver yourself. A companion volume, *Taste and See*, may be helpful in opening up new approaches to personal prayer for you.

And whatever form of prayer seems helpful, make it a joyful habit to stop for a few moments each day and notice something, or someone, who has revealed some aspect of the mystery we call God in the course of the day. This habit can become a lifestyle, and it can be the nudge that moves us on to a new stage in our growing closer to each other and to God.

One day at a time

When you are adrift, you are in survival mode. All your energies will be needed to keep yourself afloat, and to harvest the fruits of the drifting time (as we shall discover later). Energy is at a premium, so use it well and focus it carefully.

We know, from the many hostage stories that have come to light in recent decades, that one important survival strategy for people who are, as it were, under siege is to keep their minds focused. Some invent complex mental exercises or memory games, and most find it important to keep track of the passage of time. All these strategies seem to be about focusing, and prevent the mind, under such stress, from disintegrating into breakdown. When we are spiritually becalmed, we might find similar strategies helpful to focus not our minds, so much as our hearts. Where energy is limited, we need to focus it on what is truly the most important thing.

Reflect

You might translate this into an invitation to ponder questions such as:

- *Where is the real and central focus of my life? What would I want to be remembered for?*

- *What really matters in my life? If my house were on fire, what would I try to rescue?*

- *What aspects of my living are leading me closer to God and the true center of my being, and what are tending to lead me further adrift? How can I nourish the former and work against the latter?*

You will have your own versions of what the Big Questions are for you. When the waves are tossing *Rubber Ducky* aimlessly across the ocean, or when the glassy sea and breathless air cause you to grasp at quick solutions, keep coming back to these, your big issues (however you define them). This may be the perfect time to reflect on them deeply, rather than seeking desperately for ways to move away from the empty spaces.

The fruits of helplessness

When my daughter was small, I had to learn to walk slowly, at toddler's pace. To my surprise, I began to see our surroundings in a fresh light through her eyes. She had the power to bring me to a complete standstill while she inspected a molehill or a butterfly, and I began to see these things too, as if for the first time, with a child's wonder. That was, of course, if I could free myself for five minutes from the chafing anxiety about how I really needed to be back home to make that urgent phone call, or how the shops would be closed if we dawdled around much longer. Children can make you stop, as surely as a broken boat or a total absence of energy. And stopping dead can open your eyes to hitherto unseen fruits on life's trees.

And I remember one afternoon when I had made a list of all the tasks I must achieve before nightfall. The first was to post a letter. It was just the beginning of springtime and the outside world was so inviting. I took the slow option and walked across the fields to the post office, instead of getting in the car. As I dropped my letter in the box, an elderly man engaged me in conversation. I was polite, but not exactly encouraging. The list was nagging at me, and I really needed to hurry home. "Are you going far?" he asked. "Just up the hill," I replied, already halfway through the gate. "We must be neighbors," he smiled as he came alongside me, glad to have found a companion for the (for him) long and painfully slow walk back home. And so we walked. There was no alternative. To have left him standing would have been unconscionably rude. And as we walked, he told me about his life and the many interesting places he had lived. About his career as a physicist and his love of music-making. About how the town we now lived in had looked seventy years ago. As we got back to the estate, he told me about my own neighbors, people I had never made the time to get to know. As I listened to him, these other people came alive for me, as, indeed, he did himself. They had been just so many blurred faces, glimpsed hastily in my rush through life, always with one eye peering into tomorrow and the other squinting back to yesterday. Now, under his tutelage, I could see them as real people with real stories. By the time we parted, I was genuinely grateful for the way he had hijacked my quick dash to the post office. I had been grounded by him, in one sense, yet I felt the afternoon had been truly lived.

It made me reflect on the curve of my own life—both my inner and my outer life. Suppose I could plot a graph of the high spots of my visible life in the world, and of the growth spurts in my spiritual life, would there be any correlation, I wondered? I thought back over those inner growth spurts, and I discovered that, without exception, they mapped not onto my peak achievements, but onto the times and experiences when I was "down and out," when the boat was broken and the fuel drained. It has been at such times that I have discovered what it means to go deeper, to draw on resources beyond my own, to be still and let God be God in my life. And that has been the root of all growth.

It was many months after this incident that I learned by chance from a friend that the world "saunter" derives from the Latin *sancta terra*, meaning "holy ground." This wisdom prompts me to seek the grace to stop my personal race with time every so often, and, instead, just to saunter through the holiness of life's landscape.

So I urge you, when you are becalmed, not to switch over immediately to the emergency diesel engine and head for the nearest marina, but rather to try letting things be for a while, and let down your nets in the waters where you find yourself stranded. There may (or may not) be a huge catch waiting there in the depths, but the time spent simply waiting for whatever may happen next will be time spent with God.

Floating darkly

Sometimes there is simply no apparent reason for a spiritual becalming. Nor is there any apparent way of dealing with it. The old certainties that supported us in earlier stages of our journey can disappear alarmingly, just as the props supporting a ship in dry dock can, and must, be knocked away to enable a launch or a relaunch. Such an experience can plunge us into a terrifying sense of bewilderment.

The more I ponder this kind of experience, both for myself and alongside others who are going through it, the more it reminds me of a kind of birth process. We can find ourselves—often more than once in our lives—in the darkness of what we might regard as a womb. We are stuck there. In our own strength we simply are not going anywhere! Yet that darkness is also a source of life and growth, however frightening it may feel. We have no idea where our food is coming from, or what it is that holds us in being. What name can an unformed fetus give to the mother who bears her? By what name shall our souls call God?

And yet the time will come when the dark, passive emptiness of the womb turns to turbulence. All the old certainties dissolve.

The womb that sheltered us expels us. The familiar food supply is abruptly severed. It's time to move on. Perhaps our lives are a series of births and rebirths, into every new experience and stage of growth, demanding a continual surrender to uncertainty and a readiness to let go of the old handholds and trust the darkness that alone will reveal the new.

Search and rescue

The TV documentary reconstructs a tense sea rescue, off Southampton. A girl is trapped in an airlock in the submerged hull of a trimaran and the lifeboat is on its way. The documentary focuses on the girl's feelings, and on her relationship with one of the lifeboat crew who tries to be alongside her throughout her ordeal. A crucial decision has been made not to hack through the hull of the boat and get her out by force, for fear of harming the girl trapped inside it, or of causing a sudden inrush of water that could drown her before anyone would be able to reach her. Instead the lifeboat crew has decided to tow the crippled wreck to calm water, where divers will be able to bring the girl out to safety. This decision will prolong her ordeal by a further two hours, but it is considered the safer option.

Imagine, if you can, how she might be feeling, trapped in a pocket of air underneath a wrecked boat, in a stormy sea, and powerless to do anything to help herself. Feel her fear, and notice those moments when she wants to call out: "Get me out now, however you do it, whatever the risk!" Have you ever hurled pleas like that at God, begging to be liberated from some imprisoning situation in which you feel trapped and helpless?

But the girl keeps restraining her panicked desire to be free at all costs, and this happens mainly because of the calming influence of the lifeboat man, who is trying to think himself into her situation, and offer her reassurance.

If you feel trapped yourself, maybe let God do this for you (perhaps through the presence of a trusted friend): being alongside you in your plight and in your feelings about it, assuring you that it may be wiser to tow you to safety than to rescue you instantly from your captivity; encouraging you to trust the long-term wisdom rather than the quick fix.

The air in the air pocket is growing more stale every moment. The girl is struggling, and from time to time she goes under the water. The lifeboat man hears her spluttering and her silences. He keeps talking to her. He accompanies her surrender. He too is trapped in his helplessness to rescue her. And the struggle is not over when the lifeboat, with the trimaran in tow, reaches shallow waters. The hum of the engine ceases. There is a new stillness. There is a tense waiting. Home, but not yet dry. Now the girl must be persuaded to make the dive down into the depths, in order to get free of the submerged hull of the trimaran. Her rescuers instruct and encourage her: "You must hold your breath and risk the dive," they tell her. A diver is on hand to help her. But for her the dive is fraught with unanswered questions. The only certainty is that the dive will take her into deep, dark, cold and unknown waters. She must leave the relative "safety" of an air pocket in a wrecked boat if she is to discover the real security of dry land.

Twice the diver tries, and the girl gives it her best, but her best isn't good enough. She panics, fighting for breath, and then retreats, gasping, back to the air pocket, back to the old familiar prison. But on the third attempt her rescuer is stronger than her fears. He grips her and pulls her down into the darkness. Without this "death" there can be no hope of "rising." The darkness has to be plumbed, without any evasions.

The girl is everyone. The girl is me.

After minutes that feel like centuries, the rescue bid is complete. The diver brings me to the surface, and on the quayside the crowds are watching, rooting for me, praying for me, infusing me with their collective strength. They may yet go away disappointed. I may yet be carried away on a stretcher, a blanket over my head. Nothing is certain. Salvation cannot be taken for granted. But there is hope.

A huge tidal wave of fresh air floods my lungs and intoxicates my senses. Vaguely, through the daze, I hear the cheer rise from the crowds waiting on the quayside—all those who care about me, pray for me, hold me when I can't hold myself. I gasp. I laugh with an hysterical joy. My adrenalin goes over the top and I sink into a heap of helpless thankfulness, like a coil of spent rope, on the deck of the lifeboat. Someone wraps me in a blanket and carries me to dry land, and somewhere in the hazy distance there is great rejoicing over the one who was lost and is found.

Reflect

Does this incident remind you of any periods of your own life when you were inwardly trapped and helpless in a stagnant or dangerous situation? If so, try to enter into this story with the girl trapped in the trimaran, as I did myself when I first saw the documentary. Become aware of your own feelings, and of the lifeboat man encouraging you through your ordeal, and the diver pulling you down into the terrifying darkness, in order to bring you back to life. Notice the crowds—the people who are there for you personally. Notice your feelings when you take that first breath of new life.

Or, perhaps, you've been stuck in that fetid air pocket for what seems like all your life—maybe trapped in chronic debilitating illness or an abusive situation from which there seems to be no escape. Perhaps there are no crowds encouraging you, and no lifeboat man to reassure you. Perhaps, as we say in Yorkshire, there is "nobbut God." "Holiness" may not be found only in reaching port or being rescued, but also in patient, trusting, persistent pushing along against the odds. I have been blessed by knowing several such people. They are lighthouses on my own journeying!

The death of God—breakdown or breakthrough?

The Passover Feast in Jerusalem that year was to change the world. A different kind of sacrificial lamb was about to be slaughtered. The radical rabbi from Galilee had spoken his truth too clearly to be ignored any more. The world of falsehood was closing in around him. We read about these crucial days in Luke's Gospel, chapters 22 and 23.

As I read and reread Luke's description of these familiar events that we have all know about since our earliest days, I sometimes imagine a great iron chain being forged—the chain that holds us captive as surely, and even more aggressively, than the doldrums of our living or the sands and rocks upon which we run aground. We can watch this chain being forged, link by link, in Luke's narrative. We can observe how Jesus allows this chain to be forged around him, until, like a boa constrictor, it squeezes his life away and leaves him entombed in a stranger's burial cave. But, more importantly, we can engage with this same process in our own lives, recognizing and acknowledging those aspects of ourselves and our lives that are, apparently, draining all our vital energy and entombing us in our own kind of captivity.

Reflect

As we look at the links in Jesus' chain of death, read the Gospel account for yourself, and notice what these "links" mean for you.

- *The poisoned chalice:* as he gathers round the table to celebrate Passover with his friends, Jesus already knows that one of them will betray him. When friendship is betrayed, and those we trusted let us down or work actively against us, we know the bitter taste of treachery. In what ways have you experienced the killing power of betrayal in your own life? Have you ever been the betrayer?

- *The pain of being misunderstood:* imagine these close friends, gathered for the most important meal of the year, and with every kind of threat hanging over them; yet what happens? They begin to argue over which of them is the greatest! Meanwhile, Jesus, who knows what lies ahead, for himself and for them, sits and listens. Imagine his feelings. Listen to his response, "The greatest among you must behave as one who serves all the others." When, in your own experience, have you found yourself at odds with those closest to you, when there appeared to be no connection between what you were trying to express and what they were hearing?

- *The agony of isolation:* with his chosen companions Jesus walks to nearby Gethsemane and begs them to keep watch with him through his loneliest hours. They fall asleep. He sweats blood and tears, entreating God to let there be another way, but God appears not to hear him. Be present, in prayer, to any times when you have beaten at God's door, apparently in vain, and to the times when friends you so badly needed simply couldn't face the pain you were in.

- *Arrest:* the very word conjures up an image of sudden stalling and the abrupt termination of everything we hope for. Feel the rising sensation of total helplessness, the enforced movement from active ministry to passive suffering. Recall any events in your own life that "arrested" you like this. What happened to pitch your own heart into "cardiac arrest," from which there seemed to be no hope of resuscitation?

- *Denial:* the man who only hours earlier had vowed undying love now claims never to have set eyes on Jesus. Fear is the great killer of love, and Peter has fallen into the jaws of fear. Has anyone ever "cut you dead"? Or have you denied involvement with a cause or a person because of your fears? If so, simply acknowledge it, remembering that it was not the end of Peter's friendship with Jesus, but only a growth point in their relationship.

- *Mockery:* the man who, more than any other, walked the paths of this world with God, dispensing God's own love and healing and freedom to the creatures of this planet, finds himself the butt of coarse mockery and abuse. Have your most dearly held ideals and dreams ever been trampled in the mud of other people's scorn?

- *Trial:* false allegations, trick questions, hidden agendas, and secret motivations, these are the "barristers" who cross-examine the Son of Man. They did so two thousand years ago, and they do so still today, in and through us and our collusion with all that is life-denying. Have you ever felt you were tangled up in this kind of trial, when anything you said would be twisted and used against you, or when you knew full well that you were being made a scapegoat for evils that lay much deeper than anything you could give a name to? Are there any ways in which you are implicated in putting others "on trial"?

- *Institutional brutality:* for hundreds of thousands of men, women, and children, brutality is the only relationship on offer with those around them. Behind closed doors, at home, or in other supposedly safe places, they are held captive, abused, and tortured, their bodies, minds, or spirits broken, their existence annihilated. Jesus enters into this fact with his whole being. In his own body, mind, and spirit, he allows God to be put to death. He offers no resistance except the power of Life. Where do you see the evidence of institutional brutality—either gross or infinitely subtle—in the world around us? What incenses you most? What power of Life do you find in your own heart with which to offer resistance?

These are some of the iron links that are still being forged today into the chains that lock us into evil and destructive behavior and hold us captive in self-serving systems that feed on the suffering of others. You might like to ponder the precise nature of the links that make up your chain. The Gospel doesn't allow us to take the easy option of claiming instant release! Jesus himself had to die and be buried. He had to descend into the bottomless pit of despair.

Chains like these can drag us down to the depths of helplessness. But the story of Jesus' last hours, and their aftermath, reveals a deeper meaning. The chains that hold us captive can be the very same chains that can lead us to the depths of ourselves, and to the discovery, in those depths, of the bedrock that will hold our tossing ship with a steadiness that we could never have reached from our own resources. They can become anchor chains. It may feel like a total breakdown, as indeed it did for Jesus, but if we can drop that chain overboard, it may become the means of our breakthrough to a new level of being.

Reflect

Look again at the links in the chain that holds you captive. Name them and bring them, one by one, to God for healing and liberation. When you are ready, throw your chain overboard, and let it sink down to the depths of your being and take hold in the bedrock of all being, who is God. Drop anchor, as Jesus dropped anchor on that first Good Friday, trusting, in the darkness, that there is a bedrock that will hold you and will ultimately be the source of your eternal Life.

CHAPTER

7

Dropping Anchor—Moving On

When we can do nothing else to help ourselves, we can drop anchor—that is, of course, if we remember that we have an anchor to drop! For myself, I know too well that I can become so embroiled in the nitty-gritty of everyday life, and so preoccupied with the various storms that blow up in my path, or frustrated by the spells of being stuck in a rut, that I can easily forget the importance of the "anchor." But what kind of an anchor really makes sense in our voyaging? Where do we find it, and how do we use it?

The chapter title captures something of the paradox of our inner journey—the need both to be still and to continue the voyage, to drop anchor and yet to journey on. In this chapter we will try to unpack this paradox a little and reflect on what it means for us to find and use the right anchorages, and to have the courage to weigh anchor and journey on when the time is right.

Safe havens?

One of the more unfortunate metaphors that we use to express our sense of "heaven" as our ultimate destination, is that of the safe haven. It's not hard to understand why we have alighted upon such an evocative phrase. Given the turmoil and stresses of most people's lives, what could one wish for more ardently than a safe haven into which we might steer our battered little boats at the end of the race? So is that all it is—a touch of wish fulfillment? I think of the girl trapped in the submerged trimaran in chapter 6, or the homecoming of round-the-world solo sailors like Ellen MacArthur on completing the Vendée Globe race, and the roar of the crowds lining the harbor to welcome them home makes me long for such a triumphant homecoming where eternal safety is grasped from the jaws of potential disaster. Perhaps our whole emphasis on the doctrine of salvation feeds our longing for such ultimate safety, where there will be peace and justice, light and love.

These may be the pivotal images we cherish of heaven, and it is no surprise that we find a deep disconnection between such dreams and our lived experience in the here and now. So we do the natural thing, and we seal off our heavenly dreams into the Sunday slot, and try to prevent them from being submerged in the angry oceans of our Monday to Saturday world. However bad things are, we are steering toward a safe haven, we believe. The destination will blot out all the bad memories of the struggle of the voyage, right all the wrongs and reward all the rights.

Conscious of this deep dream for the safe haven, our next step might be to establish earthly replicas of it where we can pass our time in relative peace. The sailing fraternity does this on a grand scale, and they call their replicas marinas. It is said that a high percentage of sailing craft never actually leave the marina, or, if they do, make only quick trips out into familiar waters and return before nightfall or stormfall to their permanent moorings.

But there are others who want to venture into deeper and more challenging waters. They may undertake longer trips, involving overnight stops or other periods of rest. Such craft may take advantage of fixed moorings, allowing them to tie up to a fixed point of relative safety, usually close to the coast, marked by a buoy with a mooring ring.

But those who long to voyage freely in uncharted waters will have to carry their own anchors. If you know how to use your anchor you can sail where you will and stop as and when you need to. You could compare the marina to the hotel of the boating world, while the mooring is more like a bed-and-breakfast stopover, and the anchor gives you the freedom of the backpacker.

How does this relate to our Christian voyaging? I invite you to draw your own connections. I know that I personally have needed, and still need, the faith community and collective safety and sense of identity of the marina, but that I am actually happier when I can chug along the coastline, choosing my own moorings, sharing a living encounter with those I chance to meet along the way and participating in their expression of their faith before moving on. And I know that there is the loner in me who needs that solitary anchorage of quiet prayer in the midst of whatever life throws at me and that this doesn't depend on the proximity of a marina or any fixed moorings.

These reflections raise the question in my mind: is it really safety that I am looking for when I search for moorings or anchorage? If safety is all I want, why would I ever venture forth from the marina? And if heaven is just a glorified marina, is that where I really want to be? When I think about these things, I realize that what I desire more deeply than safety is the challenge of the voyage itself, and the deepening, transforming power of that journey when I make it with God, who is both my boat and my ocean. To ask for a safe haven might be to close off the possibility of that venture into the ocean of God's love, and when I read the Gospels, I see nothing there about a promise of safety.

Reflect

What do the images of the marina, fixed moorings, and anchor points mean for you? How do you feel about the tension between the desire for safety and the yearning for new discovery?

Dropping anchor

If you are reading a book of this nature, you are obviously not tied up in the marina. You are under sail, and you will know about your anchor and how to use it. I have two types of anchor on my own boat. The first is prayer and reflective living. The second is those special people who are soul friends to me.

The anchor of prayer is one I need to use regularly and frequently. When everything goes well, I need to use it to come to stillness and remember who I am, and with Whom I am journeying. When everything goes pear-shaped, I need to use it to rediscover perspective and regain a sense of proportion and relativity. The bad news is that when things are going well, I often don't take the time to stop and take stock or reconnect to the core of my being because I am too busy trying to gain ground and win the race. And when things are going wrong, I am too preoccupied with fixing them to have time to consult that deep inner compass. So I am at risk of forgetting how much I need my anchor, or even forgetting where it is and how to use it.

The anchor of soul friendship, or human spiritual companionship, gives me the priceless gift of being able to find a still center of nonjudgmental connectedness with someone who knows me and accepts me just as I am and will gently reflect back to me what it is I seem to be trying to do, and who it is I am longing to become.

Bobbing at anchor, in prayer and reflection, or in contemplative conversation with a soul friend, I see things differently. I see my own horizons, unobstructed by the clutter of my lesser concerns, and I feel the rope reaching down to the bedrock of my being. My own center of gravity reconnects with the center of gravity of all being, whom I call God. The axis of my own little world is, at least for a while, in right alignment with the axis of all creation, and therefore, potentially, in right alignment with all God's other creatures.

This isn't safety, in the sense of a temporary shelter from the struggles of life. This is the most real thing I am capable of touching and experiencing. If anything is eternal, this is surely a glimpse of that eternity. It isn't an escape route from the struggle but a still point right at the heart of things and the only place where the struggle falls into place and from which it can be lived out. It offers security, but only because it leads us into the core of life where all the hazards around us are seen to be relative to the absolute center "in whom we live and move and have our being." It doesn't change the outer facts. It changes, dramatically, the inner perception of those facts, and opens up new and transformed ways of reengaging with them.

Reflect

Who or what are your anchor points in life? Are you an anchor for anyone else?

Change and changelessness

Anchorage like this also reminds me that my being is, in some respects, as restless and impermanent as the ocean upon which I bob about. I have heard us described as "temporary arrangements of molecules" constantly in flux amid the quantum soup of the universe. We know that our physical being changes all the time, and that our configuration of cells is recycled completely over seven years. We know that our minds are the receptors and transmitters of constantly changing pulses of thought and feeling. Yet when I meet an old friend after long years of absence, I not only recognize him, but I find we can pick up where we left off and nothing in the depths of our relationship has changed, but only grown and strengthened. There is a constancy amid the flux. There is something deeper than the flux, something that transcends it, yet, mysteriously, is rooted within it. For me, to be at anchor is not to be safe, but it is to know both the flux and the constancy and to be at home in each.

Sailing wisdom can teach us more about dropping anchor. I was surprised to learn, for example, that it isn't only the anchor itself that holds you steady, but the weight of the chain along the seabed. How strong, I ask myself, is my chain, and how solidly does it lie on the ground of my being? The anchor chain at sea needs to be at least three times the maximum depth of water in which you intend to drop anchor, and preferably more than this. So to moor in a five meter depth of water, a chain of at least fifteen meters is needed. This reminds me that dropping anchor demands real depth, and that the strength of the connection between me and my anchor is what matters. A few shallow prayers won't hold me, and nor will a superficial relationship, whether with God or with a soul friend. And the further I venture into deep waters, the longer and stronger my anchor chain needs to be. I don't want to sit in the marina all my days. I want to sail the high seas. How can I lengthen and strengthen the anchor chain?

A few possibilities come to mind:

- I can deepen my prayer by letting God be its source, rather than relying on my own ability to express myself in words. This may lead me into simple silent contemplative presence, trusting that God is active in the depths I cannot plumb. Or it may challenge me to become the answer to my own prayers for peace and justice, by putting my energy and my resources where my mouth is.

- I can deepen my relationship with God by recognizing that God is the permanent reality that alone makes sense of the "temporary arrangement" that appears to be "me" and the turmoil of conflicting circumstances that constitute the oceans of my living. I can do this by actively seeking "God in all things" and becoming daily more tuned into the ways in which creation and lived experience reveal the nature and actions of God in every moment and encounter of my life.

- I can deepen my relationship with trusted soul friends by risking revealing more of myself into their confidence. The more they know of me—the real me—the further we can go together in discovering that alignment between my own desires and God's deepest dream.

So there are ways of adding new links to that all-important chain that has the power to connect our tossing surface lives with the ground of our being, far below our deepest levels of consciousness.

As for the anchor itself, it needs to be able to grip whatever terrain you are sailing over. At sea this may range from sand and mud to hard rock or coral reefs. These who know about these things tell us that anchors bury themselves most efficiently in sand, mud, and shingle; a seabed of rock or weed presents more difficulty and a heavyweight anchor may be needed in these conditions. So, if we regard our prayer as the anchorage of our spiritual lives, we need the kind of prayer that is possible wherever we find ourselves. Sometimes the seabed will offer an easy grip—for example when we are elated or full of gratitude and overflowing with a sense of the holiness of our world. How easy then to drop anchor and bask in the stillness of prayer! But not so easy when our circumstances feel like hard rock or when our lives feel choked up to suffocation point with the weeds of complications and dilemmas. A heavier-duty anchor may be needed then—the kind of prayer that has the courage to throw the book at God if need be, to express how we are really feeling with the vigor and violence of the psalmists or with the frustrations of Job. And that other kind of anchor—the human soul friend—is an indispensable gift in these circumstances.

Perhaps the main thing to bear in mind is that the anchor, whatever form it takes, is part of the boat, integral to the journey, ready to hold us in balance, whatever the terrain. It travels with us. Our connection to the bedrock is always there, and can be activated whenever and wherever it is needed.

Sailing on

The only trouble with anchors is that they can grow roots! We need the still point of rest and restoration that our anchor offers, but we also need to be able to let go of the mooring and set sail again. We must let go of every signpost and journey on. We cannot be "established."

Archbishop Helder Camara has this to say on the subject:

Pilgrim
when your ship
long moored in harbor
gives you the illusion
of being a house;
when your ship begins to put down roots
in the stagnant water by the quay
PUT OUT TO SEA!
Save your boat's journeying soul
And your own pilgrim soul,
Cost what it may!

The safety that we think we are seeking in our moorings, and that we hope to eternalize in heaven, is not, it appears, the final destination. Helder Camara is passionate in his warning that to stay safe may cost us the very soul we are seeking to save.

Less dramatically, but rather movingly, a Welsh couple I heard about bought a new home. They were discussing what name they should give it. The first suggestion was the Welsh word *cartref*, meaning a final anchorage, a place where one has arrived and can unpack and settle down. But their final choice was the Welsh *arosfa*, meaning a midway halt, a drop-in place where there is warmth and welcome, but no ultimate permanence.

We are on a journey. We don't know the destination. All we know is that the boat sails on and that the earth is a globe, not a tabletop. And so we might envision our life as something of a circular journey—a voyage "round the world" of our own unique circumstances—a voyage that may seem to keep on returning to its beginnings. Each return to home port carries a new degree of awareness and maturity. The circular pattern of our living reveals itself to be more like a spiral, and every choice we make helps to determine whether, in the final analysis, our personal spiral is leading upward toward the fullness of everything we are called to become, or downward into disintegration.

Perhaps the destination is nothing more, or less, than the ocean of God's love with its potential to transform us from the partialness of who we are now into the fullness of all creation into which we are being called. To live a life of faith is to trust the journey and to shape our choices in favor of the spiral that leads to Life.

A spiral voyage

It can be dispiriting as we approach the later years of life to feel that we are coming full circle and returning to the dependency of childhood, our faculties impaired, our usefulness outlived. It can feel like returning to the start line, with nothing to show for the years in between. The spiral tells us a different story. It reveals that all our experience is contributing to a process of evolution. Our choices that are life-giving and grounded in love help the spiral of our becoming move upward. Our life-denying choices and those grounded purely in self-interest drag the spiral down.

In her book *The Mystic Spiral*, Jill Purce recalls how just a faint hint of a remembered scent, for example, can reconnect us to "another place and another time" earlier in our life's journey. She adds:

The amount we have changed in the recognition of this moment—this is the spiral: the path we have followed to reach the same point on another winding. All our experiences are like that haunting scent: situations recur with almost boring familiarity until we have mastered them in the light of the previous time round. The more we do this, the steeper the gradient, which is the measure of our growth. The spiral we travel round life is the means we have to compare ourselves with ourselves, and discover how much we have changed since we were last in the city, met our brother, or celebrated Christmas. Time itself is cyclic, and by the spiral of its returning seasons we review the progress and growth of our own understanding.

Our ongoing experience is not simply a series of circular tours, bringing us back to where we began, and leaving neither ourselves nor creation any the better or the wiser for having made the journey. It is a spiraling journey, revealing the windings of our own growth in understanding and wisdom and love, and, in turn, the contribution of that growth to the evolution of all creation. Thus we spiral round the years and through the generations, growing, by the grace of God, in wisdom and in stature, and every personal circumnavigation (whether it spans a lifetime, or simply the passage of time between two birthdays) reveals a new winding of our sacred spiral, and marks our growth.

On February 11, 2001, a young woman of only twenty-four sailed into the harbor of Les Sables d'Olonne on the French Atlantic coast in her boat *Kingfisher*. Until that day she had been relatively unknown, but as Ellen MacArthur crossed the finishing line of the Vendée Globe, considered to be the most challenging race of the sailing world, she became the youngest person ever to complete the race and the fastest woman ever to sail solo around the globe. Overnight she became an international celebrity. To her own enormous surprise, "*la petite Anglaise*" was greeted rapturously by hundreds of thousands of admirers along the waterfront as she headed into port after her long and exhausting solitary voyage. She tells her story in her book *Taking on the World*. Ellen herself describes her experience of three months alone on *Kingfisher*, living in such intimacy with the ocean and the skies, as a time in which she rediscovered "the real Ellen," the core of her being. Every one of our inner circumnavigations can bestow the same kind of grace upon us.

We have much to learn from Ellen's story, and the stories of others like her who have taken up the challenge to sail solo round the world. Their story reflects something of our own spiritual journey. We have already explored some of the conditions we might sail into as we make the voyage of our own lives across the mystery of God's creation. We have faced some of our worst storms and lived through the frustrations of how it feels to be stuck and unable to move forward. Now might be the time to look at our journey so far as a whole, and to notice what we can learn from all that has been, to help us sail true into the waters that still lie ahead. What, in our own experience, has made us more "real"? How much more "real" are we now than we were on the previous winding of our life's spiral, and what will the next winding reveal?

Yet this is very far from being merely an individual journey of self-discovery. It is a journey that reflects, and affects, all that exists. Our journey is bound up with the journeys of those we love, and those we find difficult, with the folk next door, and a billion strangers, with the poorest of the poor and with the whole of creation.

The pattern of creation itself is a spiral one. A revolving universe is also an evolving universe, and nothing ever happens in quite the same way again. There is growth. There is process. The earth circles the sun every twenty-four hours, but no circling is ever the same as any that has gone before. The sun itself has moved, and the ellipse traced by the moving earth is different every time. We who inhabit earth are different. With every revolution a new configuration of created life sweeps around the sun. The old die and the new are born, and those in between have moved on. They are no longer who they were yesterday, nor have they yet become who they will be tomorrow.

All our circumstances change moment by moment. Weather systems blow up unexpectedly in the shape of conflicts or emotional highs. Troughs and depressions suck us down, and favorable winds give us new impetus. Yet in all this flux it is possible to discover the steady center, to grow from that center, and to be at home in the core of our being, as Ellen discovered in the wilds of the South Atlantic.

A cradle for the kingdom

We have reached the home run of our spiritual ocean voyage, and I would invite you at this point to reflect on what we are actually doing when we put to sea with God. Imagine the globe, shimmering blue and green as the first astronauts saw it from the moon. Now move in a little closer and notice some of the agony and the ecstasy that is being experienced on that little planet. See the brokenness and the suffering, and see the hopes and the dreams. Even as you gaze, countless small craft are plying their way around the globe. Millions of human lives are struggling to keep their little boat afloat. Look down and see the lines of their journeying crisscrossing back and forth over the face of the earth. Each one, in all those millions, is unique. Each is weaving its own narrative of battles lost and won, of loving and longing, aspiring and despairing. Each is struggling through a unique combination of weather and facing its own particular configuration of hazards. Each is harvesting its own treasure, suffering its own kind of shipwreck. Each carries a cargo that is entrusted to no other.

Is it just a random tangle of interlocking circles? Look more closely, and notice those circumnavigations that have been, or are being made with God. Remember, perhaps, those people you know personally, who have journeyed with God (whether they realized it or not) and whose voyages have made a difference for all creation, in however large or small a way. Let them light up for you, like a net of phosphorescence that sets the world aglow. For every journey made in this life-giving spiritual awareness is a new thread woven into the cocoon that will give planet Earth its chance to transform into something eternal, something that reflects God's deep dream for the universe. Such journeys are weaving a cradle for the Kingdom.

One of these threads of trustful adventure tacking its way around the globe is yours. Take a look at how it weaves around this revolving, evolving planet of ours. Let Ellen, in her *Kingfisher*, be your guide, perhaps, in tracking your own journey and noticing its effects, or if you have your own favorite round-the-world sailing adventure, take that as your model. Or you may feel more comfortable with a different kind of guide on your circumnavigations, such as a young lad from the Kent marshes who went to sea in the 1950s in one of the last tramp steamers to trundle round the world, delivering cargo wherever she was sent and never quite knowing where the next port of call would be, or what to expect there. The lad recorded his impressions in old school notebooks, which have been woven into a delightful narrative called *Eight Bells and Top Masts* by Christopher Lee, giving fascinating insight into life aboard such a vessel fifty years ago.

Ocean flyer, plodding tramp

Alongside Ellen's *Kingfisher*, the superannuated tramp steamer affectionately known as *The Tramp* looks a sorry specimen, yet if we compare our own spiritual journey to a sea voyage round the world, many of us will find more to identify with in *The Tramp* than in *Kingfisher*. For one thing, we are not engaged in a race. Each of us is making a unique journey, and there is, or should be, no competition between us. None of us can ever be ahead or behind any other, since no two journeys are alike. We all begin from our own home port and sail toward that horizon that will reveal who we truly are before God, in our uniqueness. Comparison is meaningless and always destructive.

On the other hand, we can readily see ourselves as plodding from one port to the next, picking up what we need there and delivering whatever God has loaded into our holds as cargo. *The Tramp* sets out, initially, from Amsterdam in the general direction of the Far East, but in practice the voyage is subject to constant change and redirection depending on events both on shore and at sea. Unexpected weather conditions may necessitate diversions. Cargo already loaded may be resold and redirected to a higher bidder, causing *The Tramp* to be rerouted to a different port altogether. And global events can render a destination "out of bounds" for political or military reasons. In other words, those sailing aboard *The Tramp* live from hand to mouth, never quite knowing where life will cast them the next day. Their destiny is very much in other people's hands. Predictions regarding the journey are something of a joke. Tramp sailors live in the flux of circumstance, as well as with the uncertainties of wind and weather.

Another very big difference between the *Kingfisher* voyage and that of *The Tramp*, however you identify with them in your own journeying, is that the first is essentially solitary and the second is a community venture. Perhaps the spiritual journey is both of these things, and certainly I can relate to some extent with both images. There is a solitary journey going on, which challenges us to deal with our own unique patterns of wind and wave, storm and calm, and to face both the best and the worst within ourselves. It demands that we recognize that before God we are ultimately alone, with no one else to take the responsibility for our pathway through life, and no one but God to rescue us when we flounder.

Yet, though we are alone, we are also "all-one," and for most of us the journey is made alongside others. Much of the stress on board *The Tramp*, and also many of its delights, stemmed from the fact that an assorted collection of people of different backgrounds, capabilities, and expectations were thrown together in a small space over a long time and simply had to find ways of living together in reasonable harmony and focus. It sounds like the story of our lives—the challenge and stress of the workplace, the family, the community, whatever shape it takes for us. It is also worth remembering that, though the solo sailors take to the waves alone, they do so in the full recognition of their dependence on a wide range of support from others, and they do so only for a short time. While we need solitude to grow into who we really are, we also need community, and perhaps we grow most when we feel most constrained and frustrated by those around us. Evolution tends to happen when there are problems to overcome, and most human transformation grows out of the messiness and the conflicts of our interrelationships.

Reflect

Imagine yourself sailing solo round the world in your own version of Kingfisher. *In what particular ways have you been most challenged, or pitted against yourself? How have these challenges contributed toward your inner growth?*

169

Now imagine yourself sailing the world in a tramp steamer, as one of a motley crew. In what ways has this kind of collective journeying helped to shape you? How do you feel about the shape your voyage has taken so far—the ports you have called at, the cargo you have delivered, the people you have been asked to relate to?

I once heard these two kinds of round-the-world voyage compared to a typhoon and a snail, respectively. The track of your circumnavigation may feel like the vapor trail of a jet aircraft, or it may look more like the trail of an inebriated snail, yet it has delivered its cargo. It will have had its typhoon aspects, and its snail features. Both are part of the spiral journey!

Round the world—your "eighty years"

Whether your boat flies like a *Kingfisher* or plods like *The Tramp*, or, most likely, a mixture of the two, you are making your own circumnavigations and you will probably recognize some of these common features.

Reflect

Just notice anything that speaks to you in what follows. How do you remember a particular experience? In what ways did it help you to grow?

- *The preparation:* Pete Goss, in his book *Close to the Wind*, says ruefully that there are two races involved in competing in the Vendée Globe. The first is to get to the start line. The second is to reach the finishing line. Getting to the start line, for him and for many other hopefuls, proved to be the more daunting of the two. Round-the-world sailors often struggle to raise the funds they need, through sponsorship or donations and sheer hard work. Jesus warns us that it is a foolish person who sets out to build a castle and then stalls because he has failed to count

the cost. Over and over he warns his would-be fol-
lowers of the cost of discipleship. What does this
mean to you? Now that you are under sail, how do
you feel about the cost of your Christian commitment, and how, in hindsight, do you feel that God
prepared you for the journey? How might you help
others prepare for theirs?

- *The saltwater creek:* most boats put to sea by passing along a channel that connects the inland waters
  with the open seas. This saltwater creek is tidal,
  sometimes full, sometimes low, but there is always
  a channel. For each of us there is a channel that will
  lead us into the deeper reaches of our soul's journey, when the time is right. Look back to your own
  saltwater creek, with gratitude. What memories do
  you have of it? When did the boat of your inner life
  first slip out into open seas? Who helped to launch
  you?

- *First storms:* those leaving Northern Europe to set
  out to sail round the world encounter the turbulence of the Bay of Biscay. Sometimes the very first
  night of the race is spent battling with storm force
  winds. Many a sailor has passed through a very
  steep learning curve right at the beginning of the
  voyage. How were your beginnings? In what conditions have you learned the most? Our first encounter with the ocean waves of the spiritual journey
  can also, almost literally, make us feel sick—a kind
  of inner seasickness that can make us wish we had
  never set out at all. I have listened often, as other
  pilgrims have spoken of this kind of seasickness,
  and I have experienced it myself. To be en voyage
  with God can open up whole tracts of our living
  and relating that need attention, and the prospect of
  living in this new awareness can feel daunting. We
  can begin to believe that it might have been better

to stay moored in the marina than to have our eyes opened to the challenges of the open sea. Yet we also know, deep down, that there is no way back. We can't reverse our choice to set sail, any more than a newborn child can decide that life isn't a good idea and go back to the womb. We have stepped over an invisible threshold and we can't put the boat into reverse, however much we might wish we could. But the seasickness will pass. If you are struggling with it now, be assured that it won't last for ever, and like morning sickness in early pregnancy, it is a sign of new life ahead.

- *Trade winds:* eventually favorable winds will be with you. In calm and sunny weather, you may be given invaluable space to assimilate all you are learning on the voyage, and to carry out your essential maintenance. This may include, for example, taking time out to make a retreat. Often this is a period of spiritual consolation, when God feels very close and you, your boat, and the ocean are in harmony. Use the time well, to discern your course, to deepen your relationship with God and with others, to be kind to your boat and to enjoy the experience of sailing free.

- *The doldrums and the Roaring Forties:* nothing is static on this journey. You are sailing through perpetual motion and inexhaustible flux. Times of transition may pitch you into the Roaring Forties, as we explored in an earlier chapter, or the winds may subside altogether and leave you becalmed in the doldrums. Remember the times when you have hit heavy waters unexpectedly in the shape of life crises or major adjustments, or the times when you were becalmed and may even have begun to think the voyage was a figment of your imagination.

What did you learn in those periods about your life's boat and about the ocean of God's mystery?

- *Crossing the line:* a major cause for celebration on board an ocean-going vessel is the moment of crossing the equator, that invisible line that divides the northern from the southern hemisphere. At that point, as well as opening a bottle or two, and engaging in ritualistic initiation ceremonies for those who are crossing the line for the first time, sailors change their navigation system from north to south (or vice versa) and prepare to sail by a new set of charts and different stellar constellations. They also, if they are sailing north to south, leave the relatively dense land distribution of the northern hemisphere and enter vast tracts of emptiness.

In *Eight Bells and Top Masts* Christopher Lee reflects (in the words of "the lad" whose diaries he used) on the experience of "crossing the line" almost in terms of the cutting of an umbilical cord:

> It's as if everything I've always known has been untied. Until now it's been like I was on the end of a bit of string. We could sail down to the Gib, or even the Red Sea, even India, and someone could tug me back. But once you go south of the equator, it really is another world. Space, I suppose. . . . Sometimes when I've felt a bit homesick I've looked up and thought it can't be too bad because if Mum was looking up at the same time we'd be looking at the same sky. But that's not true now. I wrote to Mum and Dad this morning and told them the stars are upside down . . . this really is another world. The string's been cut.

I remember a spiritual "crossing the line" in my own journey as being the movement (fairly sudden and unexpected) from the routine observance of Christian faith to a more personal engagement with the True Life that I find incarnated in Jesus Christ. This challenged me to find new ways of navigating my heart's seas and opened up a whole new set of waymarks for me—markers that moved with me, yet always remained a few sea miles ahead of me. A more recent "crossing of the line" has been the challenge of becoming more open to other visions of truth, such as those that have evolved in the Eastern tradition. In both cases I have found myself sailing beyond the charts that have guided me in the past and entering tracts of apparent emptiness that are at once both daunting and full of promise.

When the "lad" on board the tramp steamer in *Eight Bells and Top Masts* has been through his initiation on crossing the equator, he comments: "So that's it. I suppose that means I'm real now. . . . I've been south." What experiences in your own journeying have given you the sense of having passed some very significant threshold? What has made you feel more "real"?

- *The Southern Ocean:* south of the equator (if our home waters are northern)—when we have passed our personal spiritual point of no return and committed ourselves to all its darkness and its light, what lies ahead may take on the character of the Southern Ocean—an expanse of seething turmoil, but also a place where every direction is possible. With Christopher Lee we might pause to look around. To the west, the New World and the open horizons of opportunity. To the East, the lands of mysterious otherness, and exotic adventure. Back North, the home waters, our roots and origins. But South—the unforgiving ocean, towering waves, and unrelenting winds, driving us to the ice floes. Our inner journey may lead in all of these directions, calling us into engagement with all that we are, our beginnings, our opportunities, our mystery and the intuition that our hearts will not rest anywhere short of the ultimate point, yet encountering God at every point along the way.

- *Cape Horn:* "Why go there," Christopher Lee asks himself, "unless it was to round the Horn?" And, as he comments,

Nothing was like Cape Horn at its worst . . . Wretched conditions. Magnificent seas. Superb seamanship. A combination of legends. A Cape Horner walked quietly to the bar. Nothing to prove.

Sooner or later, in some form or another, our inner journey will bring each of us to our own "Cape Horn." We probably won't ever choose this kind of challenge. Rather, it will choose us. Circumstances may precipitate us into the kind of inner struggle that will make or break us. Many people have a sense that, perhaps once or twice in their lives, there has been an experience (perhaps of serious illness or injury, a major dislocation of their circumstances, a betrayal or profound disappointment or a major crisis of faith) that has tested them to the limits and demanded the last ounce of their inner resources. We are told that the Chinese symbol for "crisis" also means "opportunity," and I know that I have sometimes clung desperately to the wisdom that "human extremity is God's opportunity."

To round the Horn alone may be to take a suicidal risk. To round the Horn with God may become our life's most powerful growth point. What does "Cape Horn" mean for you?

Yet there is a strange sense of peace at the still point in the heart of the storming. We have traveled through the worst, and we don't have anything to prove to anyone. We are becoming who we really are, and can say, with Abraham Joshua Heschel:

Just to be is a blessing. Just to live is holy.

A wild goose chase, or the flight of the Holy Spirit?

One of my treasured mementos of a retreat I once facilitated is a little "beanie" seagull that someone sent to me afterward. The seagull—her name is Loosy—reminds me of the many times in my life when I didn't know where I was going, or why, and yet the meaning in the Mystery was unfolding, in spite of (or even because of) my own sense of being lost or all over the place. With hindsight I can see such times now as times of great growth, when I had let go of the helm of my own vessel and let God do a bit of steering. I can't, and I don't want to, "fix" that kind of movement, imagining a kind of puppeteer God holding the strings of my life and making things happen. I find it much more helpful simply to notice it, to welcome it, and to try to cooperate with it, trusting that God and I are sailing the flux together in ways I don't understand. So God flies, like the wild goose of Celtic spirituality, that symbol of the Holy Spirit, across the storms and shallows of my own experience, letting the Mystery reveal itself as it will, without my knowing whence it came or where it is blowing. It's a wild flight, in the most magnificent sense of "wildness."

My little Loosy reminds me of Jonathan Livingston Seagull, the high flyer made famous by Richard Bach in his book of the same name. Jonathan trusted the spiral journey. He put all his energy into learning to fly high and to fly free, even though this caused the flock to reject him as a troublemaker who challenged them by suggesting that there was more to life than mere survival. He broke through his limits, and with every new winding he soared closer to what he understood as perfect flight. And when he had broken through the barriers of limitation, he willingly returned to the flock, to encourage others to follow him beyond the horizon of the known and the safe. "A seagull," he tells them, "is an unlimited idea of freedom, an image of the Great Gull." It is this same wildness of flight that carries our little boats around the oceans of our living, and every new circumnavigation can carry us closer to the heart of the "great Gull."

A participant on another retreat expressed this sense of journeying with God in a little clay model he made during his prayer. The model showed two strong, but gentle hands, cradling a fearfully stormy sea, painted in shades of blue, with white foam breaking across a tiny red rowing boat, tossing through the troughs of these huge waves. In the rowing boat sat a human figure, plying the oars and trusting the power of those hands that held both the ocean, the boat and the oarsman. A fragile human life at sea, but also a trusting heart at sea with God, a heart that has learned to understand the truth of Heschel's assurance that "just to be is a blessing."

Beyond the horizon

Such a sure bedrock of trust was very far from the thoughts of Mary Magdalene as she made her troubled way to the burial garden on the first day of the week, at dawn (as recounted in John 20:1–18). The Sabbath had kept her trapped into inactivity and sorrow, but now she was free to grieve for the man who had turned her life round, and revealed to her what love can mean.

For Mary, the world was still a flat earth, and the boat upon which she had pinned all her hopes had sailed off the edge into what could only be a bottomless abyss of dark and despair. She knew, now, something of what that abyss must be like. In her heart she was there too. The Dream that had fired her heart through recent years, and that had seemed to be heading for fulfillment in a Golden Age of freedom from oppression and evil, had been put to death in the most brutal and shameful way imaginable. Yes, her boat had sailed off the edge and all that remained was grief. She had brought her grief to the graveside.

The human heart does not lightly let go of its assumptions and prejudices. When we have made up our minds about something, we tend to reinvent the world to fit our expectations. So it was not, perhaps, surprising, that Mary too tried to make sense of what she found in the burial garden in terms of what she thought she "knew." Jesus was dead. The Dream was destroyed. All she could do now was to anoint the corpse of her dreaming with the tears of lost loving. But there was no corpse.

Her imagination left no space for Life where she was expecting death. Her voyaging didn't allow for the possibility that the earth might be round, and that there was no "edge." Her reaction is an echo of all human reaction to transformation, down through the ages. "I don't understand it, and therefore it cannot be so."

And so, when the man whose corpse she was searching for came up to her, radiant with life, she thought he was the gardener. Our small certainties leave little space for the possibility of a larger Truth. Mary had dropped anchor in the shallow water of human understanding. Yet in this stranger's voice she was hearing a call to weigh anchor and sail on, and risk the promise that the earth is round, and that to sail beyond the horizon may not be to sail into death, but into a new vision of Life.

Countless forests have been felled to produce the paper upon which to write all that humankind has tried to express in its search to understand this mystery. But at this moment only one word was needed. "Mary." Mary heard her name, spoken by the one who knew her fully and loved her unconditionally. She really heard it. It was a moment that changed human history, and a moment that is given to each of us.

To hear our name, to make that deep, eternal, unbreakable connection with the Mystery of God surrounding and enfolding us, and to know that this is also a truly personal relationship, is to be called beyond the horizon. It is a new "launch." Our "boat" is named by God, and launched into a voyage beyond what we think we know and understand. And it happens over and over again, because there is always a new horizon, and the voyage is a journey that spirals into infinity. We can choose to stay at anchor, for fear of the abyss beyond the "flat earth." Or we can sail on.

"Don't cling to me," Jesus warns Mary. "Don't try to drop anchor and chain us to where we are now, but trust the voyage with me, into all that we, and all creation, can become."

Ironically, the first leg of the journey beyond the horizon directs Mary straight back to where it all began—back to Galilee. But she is not the same Mary. The spiral journey has passed through a whole new winding, and the horizon has revealed a new vision.

The spiral voyage continues, each of us called to make our own circumnavigations of life. The twisting journey may appear to break us at times, and at the end of our day, our little boat, that provisional vessel, will eventually fall apart. When we are ready to voyage beyond the horizon, it won't matter any more that the boat falls apart. We will have learned to trust the immensity of the ocean of God's love.

Bibliography

On matters nautical . . .

Bathurst, Bella, *The Lighthouse Stevensons* (Flamingo, London, 2000)

Bode, Richard, *First You Have to Row a Little Boat* (Warner Books, New York, 1995)

Goss, Pete, *Close to the Wind* (Headline, London, 1998)

Grigg, Ray, *The Tao of Sailing* (Humanics, Atlanta, 1990)

Heyerdahl, Thor, *The Kon-Tiki Expedition* (Flamingo, London, 1993)

Keegan, Gerald, *Famine Diary* (Wolfhound Press, Dublin, 1991)

Lee, Christopher, *Eight Bells and Top Masts* (Headline, London, 2001)

MacArthur, Ellen, *Taking on the World* (Michael Joseph, London, 2002)

Sobel, Dava and Andrews, William, *The Illustrated Longitude* (Fourth Estate, London, 1998)

Willis, Clint (ed.), *Rough Water — Stories of Survival from the Sea* (Mainstream Publishing, Edinburgh, 1999)

Worsley, F. A., *Shackleton's Boat Journey* (Pimlico, London, 1999)

On matters "spiritual" . . .

(which means "everything," of course, but I have found the following especially helpful on some of the themes explored in this book)

Hughes, Gerard, *God of Surprises* (Darton, Longman and Todd, London, 1985)

Johnson, Robert A., *Owning Your Own Shadow* (HarperSanFrancisco, 1991)

King, Peter, *Dark Night Spirituality* (SPCK, London, 1995)

Lonsdale, David, *Dance to the Music of the Spirit: The Art of Discernment* (Darton, Longman and Todd, London, 1992)

Matthews, Caitlín, *The Celtic Spirit* (HarperSanFrancisco, 1998)

O'Mahony, Gerald, *Finding the Still Point* (Eagle, Guildford, 1993)

Purce, Jill, *The Mystic Spiral* (Thames and Hudson, London, 1974)

Shaw, Steven, *Dancing with Your Shadow* (Triangle, SPCK, London, 1995)

Sheldrake, Philip, *Befriending Our Desires* (Darton, Longman and Todd, London, 1994)

Margaret Silf calls herself "an ecumenical lay Christian who is committed to working across and beyond the denominational divides." Her own faith journey has been shaped by Ignatian spirituality, which has helped her to find real, living connections with the Gospel of Christ as a power for transformation in our modern age. She is the author of several best-selling books on the spiritual journey for the twenty-first-century Christian and is a regular columnist for America. She is based in the United Kingdom.

Ignatian Spirituality

Moment by Moment
A Retreat in Everyday Life
Carol Ann Smith, S.H.C.J., and Eugene Merz, S.J.

Drawing on the classic retreat model, *The Spiritual Exercises of Saint Ignatius*, **Moment by Moment** offers a new and inviting way to find God in our often busy and complex lives.

ISBN: 9780877939450 / 96 pages / $12.95

Paying Attention to God
Discernment in Prayer
William A. Barry, S.J.

"I am convinced," says Barry, "that we encounter God in a mysterious way and that God wants a personal relationship with each of us." Helping people pay attention to these encounters is the purpose of this book.

ISBN: 9780877934134 / 128 pages / $9.95

Opening to God
A Guide to Prayer
Thomas H. Green, S.J.

For over thirty-four years, **Opening to God** has de-mystified prayer, explaining what prayer is all about and offering techniques that ready the soul to encounter God.

ISBN: 9781594710711 / 128 pages / $10.95

Sacred Space:
The Sacred Space books are prayer guides inspired by the very popular, successful, interactive website, www.sacredspace.ie. Both the books and the site offer a way to reflect and pray each day of the year; both present a time to quietly connect with God and a space to be spiritually nourished, healed, challenged, and transformed.

Sacred Space offers:
+ Sacred Space: The Prayer Book
+ Sacred Space for Advent and the Christmas Season
+ Sacred Space for Lent

Visit www.avemariapress.com to view the most recent editions.

Available from your bookstore or from
ave maria press / Notre Dame, IN 46556
www.avemariapress.com / Ph: 800-282-1865
A Ministry of the Indiana Province of Holy Cross

ave maria press®

KEYCODE: FD912070000